HOW DOES
THE SHOW
GO ON?

An Introduction
to the Theater

THE
THIRD
EDITION

by **THOMAS SCHUMACHER**

**Producer of the Tony Award–Winning
Broadway Musical *The Lion King***

with **JEFF KURTTI**

EDITIONS

Los Angeles • New York

For information address Disney Editions, 1200 Grand Central Avenue, Glendale, California 91201.

Design by Alfred Giuliani
Illustrations (pages 7, 16–17, and 124): Scott Tilley
Previous page: Caissie Levy in *Frozen*

Library of Congress Cataloging-in-Publication data on file

ISBN 978-1-368-04937-5

FAC-025393-19221

Printed in China

10 9 8 7 6 5 4 3 2 1

Third Edition, First Printing, November 2019

This edition has been updated to include new Disney on Broadway show material.

Visit disneybooks.com

This is me in Summer Repertory Theatre's summer stock production of *South Pacific*.

Here I am at sixteen years old playing Barnaby Tucker in San Mateo Community Theatre's production of *Hello, Dolly!* I can't do this jump anymore!

This is me playing Charlie Bates in *Oliver!* The part I really wanted was Dodger.

$\mathcal{D}$isnɛy Theatrical Group

Dear Reader,

Nothing has ever brought me more joy than the time I have spent working on a play or a musical—or a piece of entertainment of any kind.

When I was a kid, my mom would play albums from old musicals on the family stereo, and the stories would play out in my mind. I'd make up the in-between parts, and the staging, and what it looked like. Years later, when I saw or worked on some of those shows, I was surprised to find out what they were really about.

"Theater" is a big concept. It is magic, it is drama, it is music. It is dance, it is beauty, it is heartbreak. It is a place where nothing is real and yet to me, it has always meant a place where everything is possible. And absolutely real. Real in my heart.

Theater has many purposes: entertainment, enlightenment, education, illumination. First, it is about creating a show for the audience. Of course, to do that you need a story written by a playwright, actors to perform it, a director and choreographer and designers to put it onstage, and—sometimes—composers and lyricists to write the songs.

It is a business, it is a hobby, it is a place to go to work, a place to play with your friends, a place to learn about yourself, and a place to learn about others. Theater can take place at school, in your garage, in a big fancy building, or even outside in the open air.

For me, the theater is a family. I grew up in rehearsal rooms and in dark theaters, sitting among empty seats and then anxious audiences, and sometimes backstage with a view of all the magic from behind the scenes. The theater is home for me, and I'd like to invite you in to take a look at what we do. Maybe you'll want to join the family, too. There's always room for one more.

It is my hope that within these pages you will find something you didn't know, something you didn't know you didn't know, and something that you'll want to know more about.

So let's begin with what seems like a simple question:
"How Does the Show Go On?"

CONTENTS

ENCORE

STUFF THAT WILL BE USEFUL AFTER YOU FINISH READING THIS BOOK

FEATURING AUGMENTED REALITY EXPERIENCES!

- Download the DisneyScan app in the App Store or Google Play
- Open the app
- Place phone camera over images inside the book identified with this symbol
- Enjoy bringing Disney Theatrical experiences to life!

OVERTURE
What Should You Know First?

What's Theater?

A theater is any space where performances take place. Plays, dance concerts, and operas all happen in theaters. A theater can be a formal building downtown or a platform in your garage or church basement. Lots of schools have theaters (sometimes these are called auditoriums) and most towns have some sort of theater building.

More than just a building, though, the word *theater* refers to everything connected with the theatrical arts—the play itself, along with the stage, scenery, lighting, makeup, costumes, music, dancing, acting, and actors. For example, when someone says, "I work in the theater," they might mean they actually work in a specific building, or they might mean they contribute somehow to producing a show. Or they are just being snooty.

Patti Murin as Anna gets some direction onstage in *Frozen* (above); *Frozen* in the rehearsal room (below).

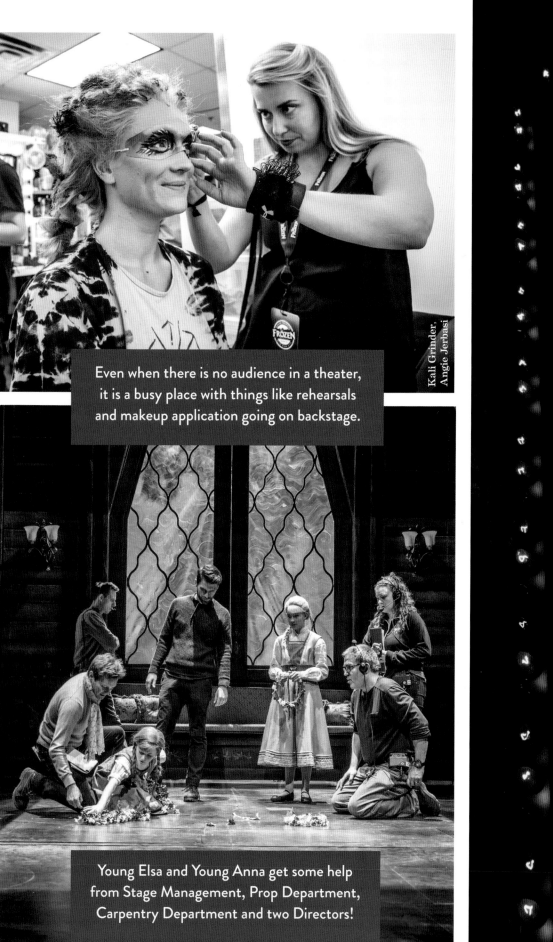

Kali Grinder, Angie Jerbasi

Even when there is no audience in a theater, it is a busy place with things like rehearsals and makeup application going on backstage.

Young Elsa and Young Anna get some help from Stage Management, Prop Department, Carpentry Department and two Directors!

BROADWAY

BROADWAY

Kinds of Shows

BROADWAY AND OFF-BROADWAY

In New York City, there are two main types of live theater: Broadway and Off-Broadway. The term **Broadway** comes from the legendary street of the same name, and a "Broadway show" is a play or musical performed in one of the specially designated theaters along or very near this street. The word can also refer to a traveling show that has once been in one of these theaters; your town may have a "Broadway series" featuring these usually famous plays that have been performed on Broadway.

    Off-Broadway means a couple of things. In New York, theaters that are smaller than a Broadway theater are called "Off-Broadway" theaters. Often, these theaters show different kinds of plays or musicals that work better in small settings, either because of the show's topic or because they draw smaller audiences.

    The longest-running play in the history of New York, *The Fantasticks*, played Off-Broadway for forty-two years!

Aladdin plays at the Prince Edward Theatre in the West End, and *Frozen* plays at the St. James Theatre in New York.

THE WEST END

    In London, Broadway-style shows are called West End shows because they are performed in the West End of London. After a while, when people see enough shows of a similar style in one neighborhood, they begin to describe the plays by that location. So depending on where you are, you might call the same type of play a "Broadway show" or a "West End show."

The Lion King opened in Shanghai, China, in June 2016.

TOURING SHOWS

A show that is successful and popular in New York or London is often restaged around the country and around the world. Sometimes these are productions that load into trucks so that the show can be seen in cities all over the United States on what is called a domestic tour. The entire production can also be loaded into boats or on airplanes to be seen all over the world. These international tours have made Broadway famous all over the globe. Putting these on can be tricky because the sets have to look big and Broadway-style, but they also need to be packed up and transported between theaters. The actors as well as much of the stage crew and orchestra also have to travel from city to city. Foreign productions need new casts and often require translations. You can hear *The Lion King* performed onstage in English, Dutch, German, Korean, Japanese, and French!

DID YOU KNOW?

The Lion King has been seen all over the world. The first time it went to Shanghai, China, on tour, we put the sets and costumes on a plane from Australia, where the show had just been performed. The same set was then loaded onto a boat and sailed to South Africa for performances there. Later we mounted it in Shanghai in Mandarin, the version of Chinese spoken in mainland China. Many of the actors were from South Africa and had to learn to speak "Chinese" especially for this production!

REGIONAL THEATERS

Regional theaters (sometimes called resident theaters) are professional theater companies located in cities throughout the United States. These theaters are very important, because they present both new plays that have never been seen anywhere else, and classic plays that may have been written more than a hundred years ago. Over the course of time, local audiences that see many plays in the same space often form a relationship with both the actors and the people who put on the shows there.

Some people like to "subscribe" to their local theater. In the same way that a newspaper or magazine subscription comes to your house on a regular basis, a theater subscription buys you tickets for a number of plays so that you can keep going to the theater again and again.

Mark Taper Forum

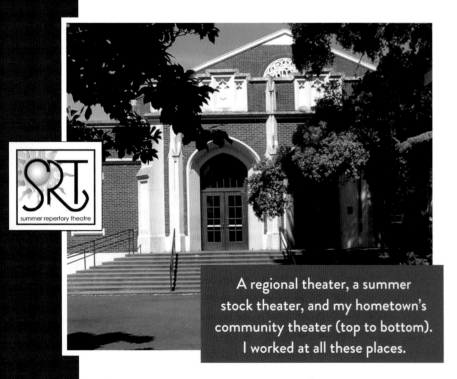
A regional theater, a summer stock theater, and my hometown's community theater (top to bottom). I worked at all these places.

COMMUNITY THEATERS

For people who love the theater, few things are as much fun as gathering with friends to put on a play. In **community theater**, most or all of the participants are unpaid, or "amateurs," which is why community theater is also called amateur theater. While some people's parents spend the weekend gardening or playing golf, others spend the weekend performing for an audience.

SUMMER STOCK

Summer stock theaters are a long tradition in America. A combination of professional, early professional, and student actors gather, primarily in resort areas, to put on classic, or "stock," plays for the local and tourist audiences during the summer months. Many of the greatest actors in the theater today got their start in summer stock productions.

Many people in theater have romantic notions about being in summer stock productions because the plays are put together very quickly with limited rehearsal time. Everyone works what seems like twenty-four hours a day to get the show on. Sometimes surprises happen right up until show time; at the very last minute of rehearsal, a star from television or Broadway might come in and play the lead!

The thrill for the audience is not only being able to see great performances of classic plays, but also to know that there is an extraordinary burst of energy in every show.

Styles of Theaters

Just like there are lots of types of shows, there are many different kinds of theaters. The main thing that makes them different is where the audience sits in relation to the stage—and there are several options.

PROSCENIUM

Probably the most familiar kind, a **proscenium** theater is where the action of the show takes place on a stage at the front of the room, and the audience sits facing the stage. A big arch, or "proscenium," oftentimes with a curtain, separates the audience from the stage area. Proscenium stages range in size from very big to very small.

BLACK-BOX

A **black-box** theater is a space where no permanent stage or seating area is built in. The stage and the audience can be set up in-the-round, thrust, or proscenium style, depending on what the director wants. This kind of theater gives complete control to each director and designer, allowing them to decide what setup will best

tell their story. This flexible theater style became popular towards the end of the twentieth century. Black-box theaters can also be built inside existing buildings, such as warehouses, or even in your own garage at home.

AMPHITHEATER

The **amphitheater** is one of the oldest kinds of formal theaters. Ancient Greeks and Romans both used amphitheaters. In those days, a classical amphitheater was built outdoors, with a semicircular seating section raised up to look down on to the stage. The Romans created amphitheaters this way because their bowl shapes hold sound very well (and microphones would not be invented until almost two thousand years later!).

These days, an amphitheater is good for music as well as plays that don't require lots of scenery. Most modern-day theaters are still shaped to naturally amplify the actors' voices, so it's often unnecessary for anyone to use a microphone.

Notice in this photo from a seat "in the round" that you see the show and everyone else watching it.

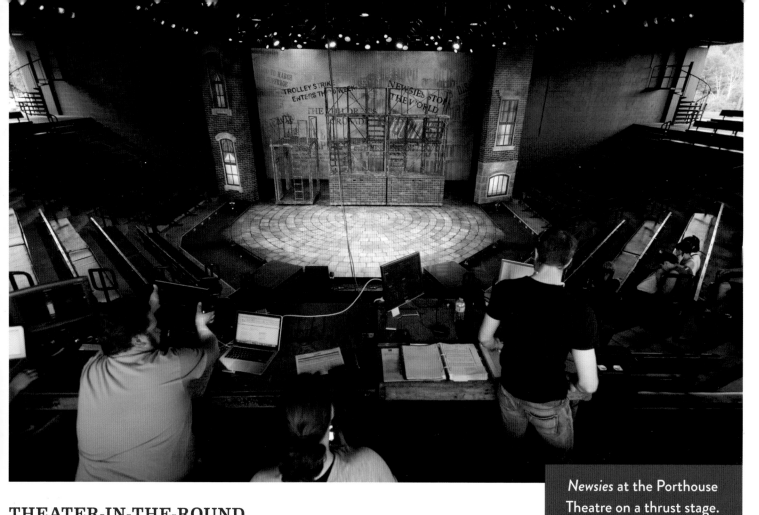

Newsies at the Porthouse Theatre on a thrust stage.

THEATER-IN-THE-ROUND

Any theater where the audience is seated on all sides of the stage is known as a **theater-in-the-round**. The stage itself can be round, square, triangular, or any closed shape, with actors entering and exiting through the audience from different directions or from under the stage. The stage is usually on the same level with, or near the height of, the front row.

Of course, having the audience on all sides can be a problem, since the actors always have their backs facing some part of the audience. However, in-the-round theater allows more people to sit close to the action.

THRUST STAGE

A **thrust stage** is like a proscenium, but with an additional piece. The "thrust" is an extra section of the stage area that extends beyond the proscenium into the audience. The thrust stage can be anything from a small extension to almost a full stage in and of itself, but in all cases the audience surrounds it on three sides.

Notice how close the audience sits to this thrust stage.

THEATER-IN-THE-ROUND

AMPHITHEATER

PROSCENIUM

DESIGNING YOUR THEATER

Here's a fun way to try out how different theaters work. Take a playing card (the ace of spades is always a good choice) and two hundred kidney beans. The card is the stage, and the beans are the people. How many ways can you organize the beans so that they can see the stage? If you put the beans in rows all on one side, the beans in the back rows are far from the card. If you put the beans in circular rows around the card, many more of the beans are close to the card. In the same way, directors must decide what kind of theater works best for their play: amphitheater, black-box, proscenium, thrust, or in-the-round.

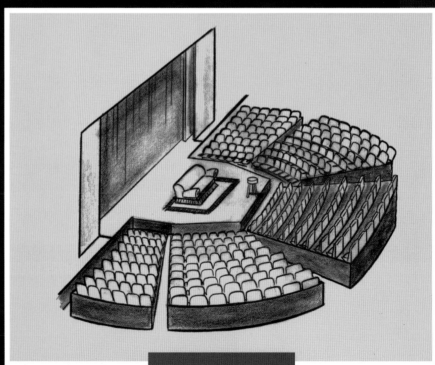

THRUST STAGE

ACT ONE Front of House:
From the Street to the Stage Apron

"EXACTLY WHAT YOU WISHED FOR!"
NBC-TV
Disney
Aladdin
HE HIT BROADWAY MUSICAL
AladdinTheMusical.com

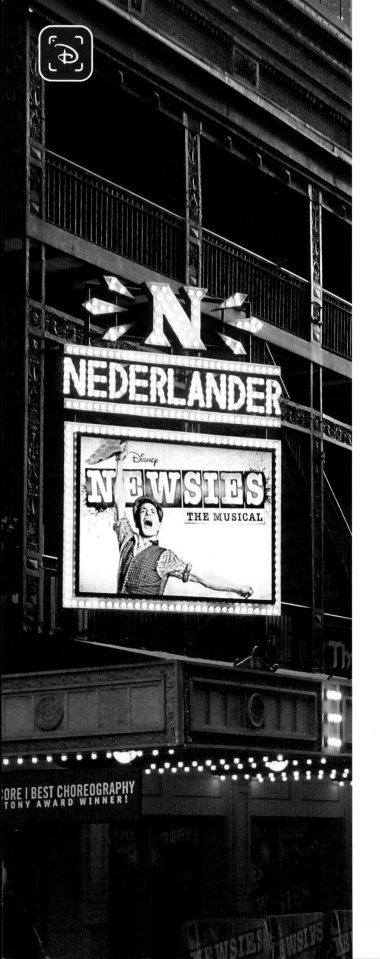

Let the Show Begin!

Most theaters are designed so that the audience's experience begins outside the building itself. Theaters are often elaborate, fanciful, or beautiful buildings meant to entice the audience and create the sense that going there is special.

On the front of the building, a big lighted signboard, known as a marquee, shows what's onstage inside. It began as a humble awning over the theater entrance, designed to keep patrons dry during bad weather. Theater owners began to attach signs and pictures to those awnings to excite audiences and alert them to special performers or performances, and as time passed the marquees became elaborate advertising statements.

Today, digital displays have come to be used on many theater marquees. Graphics, animation, and video can be incorporated into the content, and the entire "street message" can be updated or completely changed in a matter of minutes.

The expression "to have your name up in lights" means to have your name on a Broadway marquee.

What's in a Box Office?

Inside the doors of the theater building, you'll find a window, booth, or other area where tickets are sold called the box office. No one is really sure why it's called that, but people in the theater like to make up stories: here are two. Some people say it's called the box office because, historically, people may have gone there to arrange to sit in a "box," which was a special area containing several seats usually set aside for people who want to be seen more than they want to see the play. Other people believe that the name comes from when admission to the theater only cost a single coin, which was dropped into a little slot on the top of a small locked box. However the term came into use, today's box office is where people buy tickets or pick up tickets they've paid for in advance.

In the box office, the treasurer (no, not somebody hoarding a big box of jewels!) is in charge of guarding the tickets and the money paid for them, and for selling tickets to people who want to see the show.

The term *box office* can also refer to the total sales from a performance. You might ask, "How was tonight's box office?" That doesn't mean you want to know if it was cold in there or if they had fun. You are simply asking if they made much money that night.

When a show takes in more money in a given week at a theater than any show before it, the show is said to have set a box-office record. When *Frozen* opened at the St. James Theatre on Broadway, it set that theater's all-time sales records for several weeks in a row!

DID YOU KNOW?

Often if you walk up to the Box Office you can get a ticket for that night's performance for "Rush" or a discounted student price.

Traditional Broadway shows perform eight times a week, but you need to check the box office for dates and times.

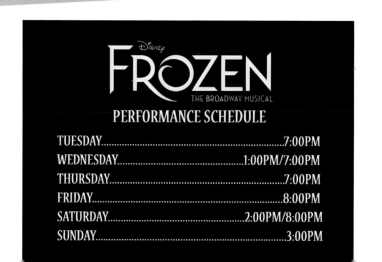

FROZEN
THE BROADWAY MUSICAL
PERFORMANCE SCHEDULE

TUESDAY	7:00PM
WEDNESDAY	1:00PM/7:00PM
THURSDAY	7:00PM
FRIDAY	8:00PM
SATURDAY	2:00PM/8:00PM
SUNDAY	3:00PM

THAT'S THE TICKET

At its simplest, a ticket is a paper receipt that proves that you have paid your admission to a play, a movie, the zoo, a museum, or even Disneyland. Theater tickets contain information such as the name of the show, the date of the performance, and often the specific place you are going to sit. Sometimes tickets are sold for any available seat, which is called "general admission," as opposed to "reserved seating," which buys you an assigned seat.

Theater tickets used to all look alike, but now they come in many different sizes. Some tickets can be printed from your home computer; those tickets have a barcode on them that ticket takers scan at the door when they let you in.

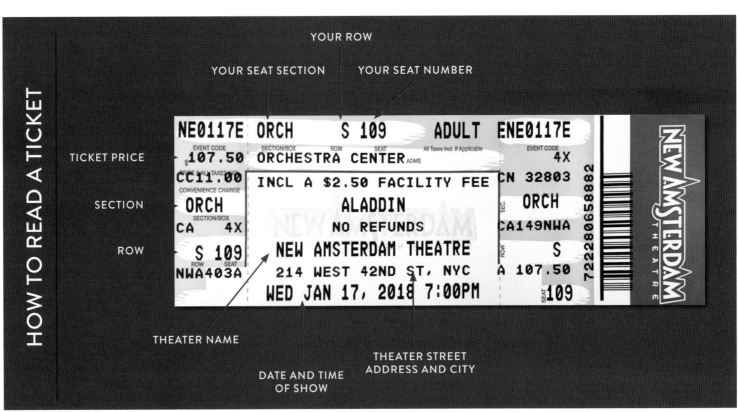

HOW TO READ A TICKET

YOUR ROW

YOUR SEAT SECTION   YOUR SEAT NUMBER

TICKET PRICE

SECTION

ROW

THEATER NAME

DATE AND TIME
OF SHOW

THEATER STREET
ADDRESS AND CITY

WHO'S WILL, AND WHY SHOULD HE CALL?

When you order theater tickets over the phone or on the Internet, you'll find them at the box office at a special window called will call. This name is short for "the place where we hope you will come and call your name so we know which tickets are yours." They usually want the person who ordered the tickets to bring their order-confirmation number, the credit card they used to buy the tickets, and a photo ID. That's to keep people from getting someone else's tickets by mistake. Ticket mix-ups can be a real mess. Sometimes tickets for the same seat are accidentally duplicated and four people try to sit in the same seat. Other times, latecomers arrive only to find that the show has started and someone is sitting in the seats they paid a lot of money for. These mix-ups can cause a major disruption or delay of the show. Sometimes they become the show themselves. Just recently, the police had to be called to a major Broadway hit because audience members began fighting over who was the real owner of the tickets!

I'VE GOT MY TICKET, BUT WHERE AM I GOING?

Ticket takers, who are stationed at entry doors to the auditorium, are responsible for checking your ticket; they sometimes tear the ticket and give back the "stub," which many people keep as a souvenir.

LOBBY

Once the ticket taker has checked your ticket, you'll pass through the theater lobby on your way to the auditorium. The lobby is a large gathering area where people can meet their friends, stand and visit with each other, find the restrooms (a great idea before every show—moms are right about that!), and often buy drinks, snacks, and souvenirs. Lobbies are also fun places to watch for interesting people. You might see some crazy types—and the crazier the show, the crazier the audience! That's part of the fun.

MAKING MEMORIES

In the lobby, you can shop for souvenirs at the merchandise counter. One of the most popular items you can buy is a souvenir program, which is a large collectible book that has many photographs of the production.

Big theaters often have tons of other stuff at their merchandise counters, like T-shirts, mugs, and dolls, to remind visitors of the show. Selling all these things is also a good way for the theater to remind people of their theater experience and how they felt about it.

Souvenir books have great photos of the show you are seeing.

HOUSELIGHTS BLINK

One of the ways you know it is time to take your seat is that the lights in the lobby will blink. This is a time-honored code that means, "We are ready to start." Another method of alerting the audience is the playing of chimes—sort of like a clock sounding. These two methods can be used before the show or at the end of intermission. If you see blinking lights or hear chimes, get back to your seat. You don't want to miss anything.

HOUSE MANAGER

The person in charge of getting everyone in the door and settled into the theater is called the house manager.

House managers oversee the ushers and ticket takers and are responsible for making sure that everyone finds their seats in time for the start of the show. Ushers are the people who greet you at the door to the auditorium and escort you to your seat. The usher will also provide a program that has information about the show, its cast, and its creators. (Programs are also good for fanning yourself if the theater is too warm!)

The house manager is also in charge of ensuring the audience's comfort and safety. The house manager uses a phone or radio headset that's sort of like a walkie-talkie to reach the stage manager backstage. A show never starts until the house manager says it's okay.

House managers are very important. Their staff is the first experience most audiences have with a show, and the better that experience, the better the rest of the show will be. "You only get one chance to make a first impression" is the rule for all good house managers. The best house managers are really good at dealing with nutty people who like to talk or take pictures during the show.

The house manager at the New Amsterdam Theatre, John Loiacono (right center), keeps everyone moving to his or her seat and is in contact with everyone backstage.

BOX SEATS

ORCHESTRA PIT

AISLE

ROW

In the House

AUDITORIUM

Once you leave the lobby and go into the seating area, you will have entered the **auditorium**. Many theater people also call this "the house." A classic expression is "The house is open," meaning that the ushers have begun seating people. Actors and technicians always want to know when the house is open so that they don't just walk out onstage or make unnecessary noise. When the house is open, the show is about to begin, so no one wants to see an actor who is in costume but not in character just pop out from behind the curtain.

The auditorium is basically a big room—often wonderfully decorated—where the audience sits and watches the show. Depending on how large the theater is, the auditorium may be divided up into different areas, and sometimes different levels. There are many names for these areas, and they differ around the world.

Aisles: The passageway between or alongside the seats in the auditorium is called the **aisle**. Similar walking paths in a church or an airplane are also called aisles, as are the spaces between the displays in a department store or supermarket.

Rows: Seats are all arranged facing the stage, usually in **rows**. Each seat in a row is numbered so you can locate where you're supposed to sit by the row letter and seat number. For example, your seat might be "Row F, Seat 104." This system helps people find the seats that they reserved when they bought their ticket.

The seating area is often sloped toward the stage (this slope is called a rake) to offer good views of the stage from every seat. Otherwise, you might just see the back of the head of the guy in front of you. And if you end up looking at the back of someone's hat, tell him, "I paid for a ticket, too!"

There's not just ONE great seat in a theater, and any seat is always better than NO seat!

The Best Seat in the House? Many people can't decide where the best place to sit is—and it is a very good question. There are many things to consider. The price of the ticket is higher for the best view of the stage. Some people like to sit higher up to see the entire "stage picture," particularly to view the staging and choreography. Others like to sit very near the stage just to see the actors' faces close up.

I like to see shows often, and I've sat in seats all over the theater. My rule of thumb is to try sitting in several locations over time. You'll get a sense of where you want to be. The most important rule is to never sit where people think you are "supposed" to sit just because it is expensive. Sit wherever you can get a seat and enjoy the play.

Downstairs: Generally in America the main floor is called the **orchestra** section. (In ancient Greece, the "orchestra" was the space between the seating area and the stage where the chorus and the instrumentalists sat. This is how the modern orchestra got its name.) In London, this area is called the stalls (in Shakespeare's time the main floor was not the best seating; in fact they didn't sit at all—they stood just like horses in a "stall").

Upstairs: The second level has many names. Sometimes it is called the **mezzanine**, sometimes the **balcony**. In London, it is called the **dress circle** or the **upper circle**. It can be very confusing, but there is always signage to tell you where to go, and your ticket always says what section you are to sit in.

Box Seats: Along the sides of the auditorium, there are often very fancy little seating areas for small groups, set aside in private balconies facing toward the audience and stage. These are called **box seats**, and although they look very cool, they are not a place to sit when you want an especially good view of the action onstage—they're more for when you want to *be seen yourself*!

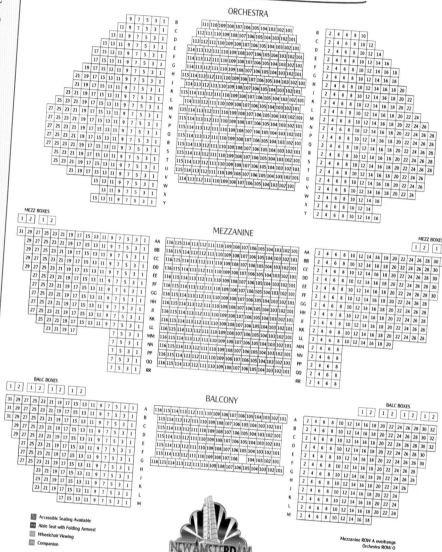

The seating chart shows exactly where every seat is. At the box office you can look at the chart and decide which seat is best for you.

Sometimes box seats have terrible views of the show, but great views of backstage. I love sitting there the second time I see a show so I can see how they do it. Stagehands aren't always interesting to look at, so I recommend seeing the show first and then looking into "the wings."

Standing Room: Many theaters have special floor space where they can sell tickets for people to stand, usually when all the seats are filled, known as standing room.

You might hear a very popular show described as "standing room only" (abbreviated as SRO), which means that it is so well attended that all the seats are taken, leaving only the standing areas. It is tiring to stand all night, but worth it if the ticket is really cheap and the show is really good!

I don't recommend it for long operas. I learned that the hard way.

SETTLING IN

Once you have found your seat, it's always fun to look around the theater and see how it is decorated, or just watch the other people in the audience arrive and find their seats. Notice how many people still dress in their best clothing to attend the theater, which is a long-standing tradition and still a fun part of the show, especially on Broadway.

As you look around the theater, you might notice certain things right away. The proscenium arch, for example, is the "frame" that separates the stage from the audience, through which the action of a play is viewed.

You'll probably notice a ledge between the curtain and the orchestra pit in front of the curtain. This is the edge of the stage, and it is called the stage apron, or just the apron. In some theaters, a mechanical lift can raise the floor of the orchestra pit to the same level as the stage, extending the stage apron further into the audience.

An orchestra pit is the area in front of the orchestra-level seats, and it's just what it sounds like: a big hole in the floor where the orchestra or band plays live music to accompany the performance.

The conductor stands in the pit, and you can usually see her head popping up as she directs the music. If there is no live music, this area is usually covered with a platform to add more seats.

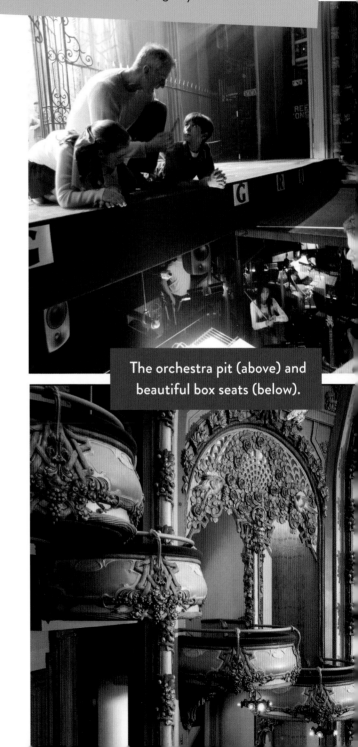

DID YOU KNOW?
One of the most dangerous things in the theater is the possibility of falling off the stage into the orchestra pit. Everyone who has worked in the theater for a long time has seen this happen. There are many safety rules about the pit, and for a good reason—it can be a very long way down!

The orchestra pit (above) and beautiful box seats (below).

SITTING PRETTY

A program is a flyer, booklet, or magazine listing the order of events and other important information, including a cast list, cast photos, cast biographies, song lists with singers' names (if it's a musical show), and a list of scenes.

The usher will usually give you a program on the way to your seat. One of the best parts of going to a show is sitting down with a fresh program and learning a little bit about what is going to happen and who is going to be performing.

Programs also make great souvenirs from the show. Some theaters have very elaborate programs with essays on the play's topic. These are fun to read after you go home.

Sometimes when you go to a show you get a Playbill. Playbill is the most famous publisher of theater programs in America, and their logo is a symbol of Broadway theater. The founder of the company, Frank Vance Strauss, thought of giving a program to the audience with information about the show and selling advertising in it like it was a little magazine. This was a very smart idea and is great for the audience because it gives them important information for free.

One of the best theater collections you can start is a collection of programs from the shows you've seen. Start collecting programs now and in a few years you'll look back and remember the shows you saw just like you were there again. I collected all the Playbills from my first trip to New York when I was in college, and those programs still remind me of the very first night I sat down in a Broadway theater. They sit in a box with programs going back to the first big show I performed in when I was in the fourth grade!

Today you can visit **playbill.com** and learn all about every show on Broadway, past and present. It is the greatest resource of actors, directors, playwrights, and all the people who make theater. Sometimes I get lost in it and just read about old shows for hours.

Who's Who?

PLAYWRIGHT

You'd think that a person who writes plays would be called a playwrite. But actually, it's spelled playwright, and it's just a coincidence that the words sound the same.

Plays are actually said to be "wrought," just like a wrought iron railing or wrought iron piece of furniture; when something is "wrought," it is heated, hammered, and bent into shape. The title "playwright" suggests that plays are hard, physical work created by craftspeople. Or it just means that playwrights want a name that is special, just like everyone else who works in the theater.

Writing plays is a particular form of writing. Journalists write articles for magazines or newspapers and report what has happened or their opinions about events. Novelists write stories in the form of books, and poets write poems to be read alone or in collections. The playwright writes the story and the dialogue of a play, as well as many of the stage directions that the actors and director follow, to tell a story for the stage. Writing a play is a bit like writing a novel, because the writer must create characters and plot. It is also like writing music, because you don't really know what you have written until you hear it performed and listen to how it sounds out loud.

In *Frozen*, playwright Jennifer Lee created specific dialogue and actions for the characters to perform and wove that into dialogue from the film version, which she also wrote. Or wrought.

Although the writer's words are usually considered unchangeable, the same is not always true for the stage directions in a script. Some directors follow them very closely. Other directors ignore them completely. (Let's let them fight about that later.) Sometimes when you read a play, the stage directions come from the original production and are specific to the original staging, scenery, and cast. You can always make up new staging, and don't need to follow what is written—though usually the people who wrote it are pretty smart and have a good idea of how you might think about it.

Jennifer Lee, the "bookwriter" of *Frozen*. She also wrote and directed the movie!

Jelani Alladin as Kristoff with Sven (above) from *Frozen* on Broadway.

Stage Notes

❄ *Frozen* playwright Jennifer Lee saw story opportunity in taking her animation screenplay to the stage. "We don't have the same special effects where it defies physics, but we have real human beings on the stage, which does a lot more," Lee says. "It affects us, I think, in a much deeper way. And I think theater—there's always a suspension of disbelief where you surrender to it."

❄ Playwright and six-time Tony Award nominee Chad Beguelin not only wrote the script for *Aladdin*, he also wrote lyrics for many of the songs.

❄ Rick Elice was on staff at Disney before he wrote the legendary *Jersey Boys*. Rick later wrote the script for *Peter and the Starcatcher*, our first show adapted from a book.

❄ David Henry Hwang does his best writing lying down, in longhand, on legal-size pads of paper. Only later does he type out the script using a computer. For *Tarzan®*, we got him a special yoga mat so he could write new dialogue and scenes during rehearsal!

Chad Beguelin wrote the book and some of the lyrics for *Aladdin*.

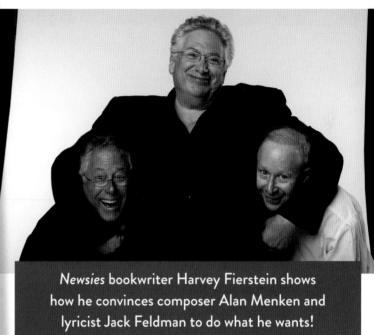

Newsies bookwriter Harvey Fierstein shows how he convinces composer Alan Menken and lyricist Jack Feldman to do what he wants!

TRY YOUR HAND AT WRITING

Playwrights have to put down on paper the way different people sound when they talk. This is called writing in a particular "voice." See if you can write a one-page scene between three people you know. Be sure to include some stage directions to capture their personalities. Don't use their real names, but show it to them and see if they can guess who is who.

Was your selection of words specific to the way they speak in real life? Did it capture their personalities? Did it surprise them that you were able to capture their attitude by writing in the way that they speak?

Tarzan® playwright David Henry Hwang reviews important script changes with associate director Jeff Lee.

DIRECTOR

"Hey! Who's in charge here?" That question gets asked a lot in life, but inside a theater everyone knows it is the **director** who is in charge.

There are all sorts of "directors" in life, and they are usually some type of boss. They may be the director of sales at a department store or on the board of directors at the local symphony or museum.

Frozen director Michael Grandage (above); *The Lion King* director Julie Taymor (below).

Directors are always in charge of something. In the theater, the director is in charge of everything that happens onstage. They don't act—the actors do that—and they don't design the sets, costumes, or lights—the designers do that—but the directors guide the cast and crew toward the goal of creating a wonderful production.

The best directors hire the best people, and they all work together to create a show that feels like it is all one person's idea, or *vision*. Some directors can also act, design, produce, or write—but every great director knows that when they are directing they need to focus on the show as a whole.

Stage Notes

❄ Michael Grandage, director of *Frozen*, was raised in Penzance, England, where his father ran a candy store. No one in his family had ever worked in show business. He started first as an actor before he became a Tony and Olivier Award–winning director.

❄ *Aladdin* director Casey Nicholaw is both a director *and* a choreographer. He was an actor in eight Broadway shows before he started to choreograph and eventually direct, too.

❄ Julie Taymor, director of *The Lion King*, has studied theater techniques and directed shows all over the world. In 1998, she was the first woman to ever win a Tony Award for directing a musical—*The Lion King*—on Broadway. That was seventy-eight years after women won the right to vote! What took so long?

❄ The best directors have a deep knowledge of every part of stagecraft, including scenery, lighting, and costumes—not just acting. Some directors are loud and bossy, and there is no mistaking who they are. Others almost whisper. The job is to get the show on the stage, and there are many ways of doing it.

❄ Rob Jess Roth, who directed the original stage production of *Beauty and the Beast*, had the idea of putting the animated film on Broadway before anyone at Disney thought about doing Broadway shows. That one idea started the entire Disney-on-Broadway business. The musical ran for more than thirteen years on Broadway and is currently the tenth-longest-running Broadway show in history. Full productions have been mounted worldwide in more than two dozen countries, including China.

Beauty and the Beast director Rob Jess Roth and set designer Stan Meyer

Newsies director Jeff Calhoun

Hercules director Lear deBessonet

Aladdin director Casey Nicholaw with Alan Menken and Chad Beguelin

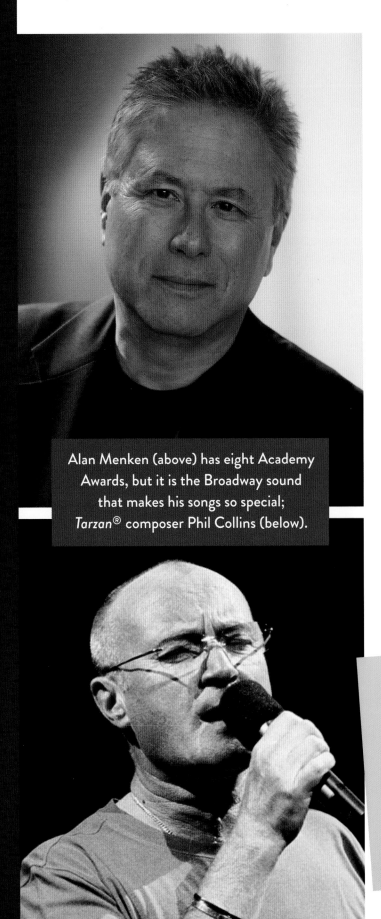

Alan Menken (above) has eight Academy Awards, but it is the Broadway sound that makes his songs so special; *Tarzan*® composer Phil Collins (below).

COMPOSER

Some straight plays have music that is played under the action or between the scenes, but all musicals are built around the work of the **composer**. Some of the most popular music of the twentieth century was written for musicals—and often the songs become better known than the shows they were written for!

Perhaps the single most important choice for a musical is who the composer will be. It may be even more important than the idea, because even some pretty goofy ideas can turn into successful musicals if the songs are memorable.

Composers write many different styles of music for the theater. They can write rock music like Phil Collins did for *Tarzan*®; they can write traditional musical theater songs like the popular ones Alan Menken wrote for *Beauty and the Beast*, *Aladdin*, and *Newsies*; or they can write what's called "world music"—a specific ethnic or regional vernacular style like Lebo M used for *The Lion King*, incorporating beautiful South African chants and songs. Some composers are great musical performers, and others can barely play an instrument. One famous Broadway composer could only hum his songs, so he sat next to someone at the piano while they figured out the notes and the chords to create the music.

The music in a show can tell you where you are, how the characters feel, and what the overall mood is. The composer of a musical is also responsible for the music played between the scenes and during dance numbers. The composer often has a musical staff to help with all of these assignments.

DID YOU KNOW?

Every composer has a different way of working. Some write tunes first, and then the lyricist fits in the words. Robert Lopez and Kristen Anderson-Lopez sometimes write while they take walks. "Let It Go" from *Frozen* was partially created on a walk in Brooklyn's Prospect Park. Elton John likes to write the music to lyrics that have already been written. The lyricist doesn't even need to be in the room. For *The Lion King*, Sir Tim Rice faxed Elton the lyrics to the song "Circle of Life," and Elton wrote the melody in twenty minutes!

Stage Notes

✳ Composer Robert Lopez and lyricist Kristen Anderson-Lopez wrote more *new* songs for the play *Frozen* than were originally in the movie, including new songs for Kristoff, who hardly gets to sing in the movie at all.

✳ Eight songs were added to the Oscar-winning score of *Beauty and the Beast* in its transition from animated feature film to Broadway. Seven of those songs were written by Alan Menken and Sir Tim Rice.

✳ There's a musical number in the stage version of *Beauty and the Beast* called "Human Again," sung by a group of characters who have been turned into household objects by a curse, where they dream of being turned back into humans. The song was originally written for the film but ultimately wasn't included. After the song became popular onstage, the film's original directors and producer completed the abandoned animated sequence for the film's rerelease on IMAX and DVD.

✳ Another "cut song" from the film *Aladdin*, called "Proud of Your Boy," was used for the stage adaptation, with two other songs written for the film by Menken and Ashman, and four new songs written by Menken and Beguelin.

The Lion King and *Aida* songwriters Sir Elton John and Sir Tim Rice (top); *Frozen* songwriters Robert Lopez and Kristen Anderson-Lopez (below).

"We are the music makers, and we are the dreamers of dreams."

Arthur O'Shaughnessy, "Ode"

LYRICIST

The **lyricist**'s job is to write the words that go with the composer's music. Sometimes the composer is also the lyricist, but many of the most famous songwriting teams split the job between writing music and lyrics.

Lyricists share the job of revealing the plot and the characters' thoughts with the playwright. Sometimes the lyricist is the playwright, too.

Lyrics are like poems set to music. They are often very beautiful even when read without any music at all. Some lyricists write the words to the song first and then give them to the composer. Other times the composer comes up with a musical idea and shares it with the lyricist, who comes up with a lyric to it. Some writing teams share the responsibility of both the lyricist and the composer, with each person dabbling in music and lyric writing. However they create the song, all that matters is whether it is any good.

Often, the lyricist has the job of turning spoken scenes into songs between two characters. Other times songs are written for just one person—as if they were sharing their inner thoughts directly with the audience.

Brilliant lyricist Howard Ashman died before his film *Beauty and the Beast* opened, but his words live on every night onstage around the world in productions of *Beauty and the Beast*, *Aladdin*, and *The Little Mermaid*.

Some lyrics change a great deal while the story of a show gets worked out. The tune can stay the same, but the lyricist, like the playwright, must keep writing and rewriting. Lyricists have to know a great deal about poetry, a great deal about playwriting and character development, a great deal about song structure—and a great deal about patience.

Ask any lyricist, and she'll tell you why that last bit matters.

Brothers Richard Sherman and Robert Sherman (bottom left) wrote songs—both words and music—for Walt Disney as a team; Anthony Drewe and George Stiles (bottom right) have been writing songs together for over twenty years! Together these four men created the songs for the stage version of *Mary Poppins*.

Kristen Anderson-Lopez, Robert Lopez

Kristen Anderson-Lopez, Michael Grandage

Patti Murin

PRODUCER

Producers have one of the hardest jobs in the theater to describe or understand. Basically, producers are the ones who decide to put on a show and decide what the show is. Then they assemble the people to do it (the playwright, director, designers, actors, and everyone else) and supervise their work. Producers are usually held responsible if the show fails but are often ignored if it is a success—except by their friends, of course.

Peter Schneider and me, with our Tony Awards for *The Lion King* (right); legendary producer Sir Cameron Makintosh and me while working on *Mary Poppins* (far right).

You may think that the director and the producer both sound like the "boss" of the theater, but the difference is that the director is the boss of what happens onstage, whereas the producer is in charge of overseeing things that need to be done beyond the stage. It is the producer's job to arrange for everything that the production will require—from staff, to rehearsal space, to a theater. The producer also oversees the marketing, the advertising, the publicity, and the ticket sales.

Producers sometimes have very strong creative ideas about the production and work closely with the director, writers, and designers. Other producers are more businesslike and supervise only the logistics, leaving the creation of the show to others. No matter what, the producer is in charge of making the show a success.

The reason why producers literally "run the show" is because they are also in charge of getting and managing the money. Producers set the budget for the show and collect the money from investors, companies, or even their own bank accounts.

However, there is much more to producing than writing a check, coming to a few meetings, and putting on a tuxedo for opening night. Producers care deeply about the success of the show, and do their best to make sure everything runs smoothly.

My coproducer Anne Quart (left); me and my producing partner for *Shakespeare in Love*, Sonia Friedman (right).

Stage Notes

❋ Legendary British producer Cameron Mackintosh started working backstage as a stage manager for the original London production of *Oliver!* In those days, stage managers also went on in the show for actors who were too sick to perform. Phil Collins (who wrote the music for *Tarzan®*, remember?) was in the show at that time, and Cameron was Phil's understudy. Nobody could have possibly known then all the great things that were to come for both of them!

❋ I went to school to pursue a career in theater. I planned to be both an actor and a director. During the final bow of the last musical I appeared in, *Pippin*, I suddenly realized that I never wanted to act again and wanted to be a producer instead. I walked off the stage, took off my wig, costume, and makeup, and never performed again. I went back to school and dedicated myself to one day having my own theater company to run, which is what I do at Disney today.

❋ Many producers are too nervous to sit down with the audience and watch a show. I can usually be found in the back of the theater pacing, or perched on stairs, or checking out the view and audience response from the balcony. Walking keeps me from climbing out of my skin!

> "All the inspiration I ever needed was a phone call from a producer."
>
> *Cole Porter*

The West End Cast of *Shakespeare in Love.*

MUSICAL SUPERVISOR AND CONDUCTOR

There are a few jobs in the theater that have more than one title. The music department is where a number of the jobs overlap. Some shows have such enormous amounts of music that there are many areas of the music to oversee. Brand-new musicals that have never been performed before are particularly complicated, because the songs, the underscore (the background music), the overture (the music before the curtain goes up), and the dance music all need to be sorted. The music played by different instruments needs to be assigned and written out, the orchestra needs to be taught the new music, and the singers need to learn what they will sing. For big shows with all these musical elements, a **musical supervisor** coordinates everything.

Often, the musical supervisor is also the **conductor**, but not always. The conductor is a person everyone recognizes. They usually stand with their back to the audience, facing the orchestra and the stage. In most theaters, the orchestra is positioned between the audience and the stage, often in a slightly lower "pit" to avoid blocking the audience's view. The conductor's job is to set the pace or tempo of the songs and keep the orchestra and the singers all performing together. From their vantage point, they can see what's going on onstage and cue the musicians when to start. Very often the orchestra can't hear the singers at all, and sometimes the singers can barely hear the orchestra, so by watching the conductor, they can tell where they're supposed to be.

This is Annbritt duChateau, the associate music director of *Frozen*.

HOW THEY WORK

Try to imagine you are singing a song with a friend but you can't hear each other and you can't see each other—maybe your friend is in the next room. How do you know when to start, or if you're singing faster or slower than the other person? The conductor is the one who keeps the music all together and sounding great. Conductors also have to have very strong arms because they wave them around all night! It can be a very strenuous workout to conduct a show—almost like taking an aerobics class at the gym.

With the front row so close, many conductors and orchestra members can carry on conversations with people in the audience before the show and at intermission.

Stephen Oremus (above) supervised the music and arrangements for *Frozen*. Michael Kosarin (below) was music supervisor on many legendary shows, including *Aladdin*.

Stage Notes

✳ Once, conductor Paul Bogaev was hit on the head with a program at the end of a show by an elderly lady who was unhappy that the leading man died in the final scene. Apparently, she didn't realize that he didn't write it, he just conducted it!

✳ Conductors get good at catching all sorts of props that are heading into the orchestra pit. If you look closely, there are often big nets (sort of like fishing nets) over the orchestra to stop stuff (and people) from falling in.

45

Choreographer Rob Ashford rehearsing a dance for *Frozen*.

CHOREOGRAPHER

The **choreographer** is in charge of the dancing in a play or a musical. Some plays have scenes where one or more characters have to dance, and a choreographer is brought in to decide what that dancing will look like. In musicals the choreographer is almost like another director, and the job is a lot of work. Every time you see someone dance in a musical onstage, on-screen, or in a music video, a choreographer has designed those movements and taught them to the dancer.

The word *choreography* comes from the ancient Greeks, who performed dances in all their plays and pageants. It literally means "the writing down of dance," but over time it has come to mean creating the dance.

Every show has different dance needs.

Some choreographers have such specific styles that you can tell immediately that a dance is theirs. Usually, choreographers will adapt their style to the needs of a

The cast of *Frozen* in the rehearsal room.

particular play, incorporating historical styles or different cultural folk dances, if that's what the script calls for.

Dance can tell a story, dance can celebrate, dance can break your heart. Sometimes the dancing is performed along with singing, and sometimes a dance is set to music with no lyrics. No matter how dance is performed, it is one of the most important parts of a musical—and one of the main reasons people come to see a show.

Garth Fagan the Choreographer for *The Lion King*.

Stage Notes

❋ Dancers sometimes advance the story in unusual ways. For *Frozen*, choreographer Rob Ashford staged his dancers all dressed in white to represent a blizzard and as a "whiteout" at the end of the show.

❋ There used to be separate dancing and singing ensembles in a Broadway chorus. Today, all chorus members are expected to be both skilled singers and dancers.

❋ Each week, *The Lion King* cast uses nearly one hundred ice packs to help dancers injured during the performance. The show may look pretty from out front, but sometimes it feels more like a hockey game backstage.

❋ Garth Fagan was born in Jamaica and is best known as a modern dance choreographer with his own company of dancers. *The Lion King* was the first Broadway musical he ever worked on, and he won the Tony Award.

Christopher Gattelli won a Tony and a Drama Desk Award for Outstanding Choreography for *Newsies*.

STAGE COMBAT AND WEAPONS

Frequently onstage, actors have to create the illusion that a fight is taking place. That fight might be between two kids in school, two guys in a bar, or twenty guys in the 1500s. They may just swing fists, they may swing swords, or they may have to shoot guns. No matter what sort of fight it is or what sort of weapons they are using, the fight director is responsible for it. Sometimes a fight can be something as simple as a leading lady slapping her leading man. But if she gets her move wrong, the leading man won't be leading anything but a bloody nose for the rest of the night.

Fight directors stage every swing, every step, every jump, and every blank bullet that comes out of a gun. Everyone who works in the theater knows that stage fighting and weapon use are special skills that require meticulous attention. It has to look dangerous to the audience, but the actors need to feel completely safe at all times.

The original cast of Broadway's *Aladdin*.

Stage Notes

✳ When it needs to look like someone is being cut with a knife, actors often use a plastic knife with a tube running inside it. The handle gets filled with fake blood, and when the actor squeezes it, the "blood" oozes out wherever he puts the knife.

✳ Every night before *Aladdin* there is a "fight call" where the actors who will participate in the fight that night have to go onstage and run through each of the moves just to make sure everything is safe.

✳ The character Les in *Newsies* has to jump into a barrel that is then thrown on its side and rolled across the stage while everyone else is fighting all around him. Joshua Colley, who played Les, remembers, "Just when I thought the barrel would never stop rolling, it did, right before the orchestra pit. It was so exciting and frightening at the same time!"

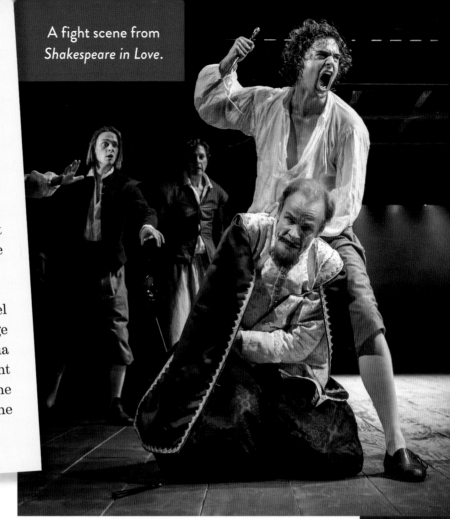

A fight scene from *Shakespeare in Love.*

A fight scene from *Newsies.*

PUBLICIST

Every show needs publicity. Usually lots of it. Publicity is free "hype" about a show—it's everything people see and read about a show that the producers don't have to pay for. For example, producers pay to have advertisements in the paper, but if the paper writes an article about the show, it's free publicity.

The more publicity you can get, the less advertising you have to pay for. That's why a good publicist can be very valuable. The publicist is in charge of creating publicity opportunities for the show. The publicist also arranges for critics to come view the show, which creates more publicity when they write their reviews.

Sometimes the publicist organizes an event—maybe arranging for the cast to make a special appearance at a store or give a concert in the park—to get the public's attention and hopefully even get a reporter to write an article about it.

Sometimes publicists put on what's known as a "publicity stunt," where they arrange for something crazy about the show to look like it accidentally happened. When *Mary Poppins* was rehearsing for its pre-London tryout, the publicist knew that a nearby academy that trains nannies

Caissie Levy (Elsa) shooting the music video of the song "Monster" (top). Elton John at the twentieth anniversary performance of *The Lion King* in 2018. Whoopi Goldberg makes a guest appearance in *Aladdin* on Broadway, all for extra publicity (right)!

was having its annual graduation. The publicist sent the actress who was playing Mary to attend the event, and it suddenly made national news and brought attention to the show, which was about to open.

Next time you read an article about something related to an upcoming show, see if you can figure out whether the event happened by chance, or if it was just a stunt arranged by a publicist.

Of course, it is usually best to get good publicity, where people say nice things about the show to build interest and encourage the public to buy tickets. However, if you can't get good publicity, terrible publicity may save the day by making everyone wonder how the heck things can be so bad! Bad publicity is never a producer's first choice.

Most publicity comes easily when a play is opening, but for plays that run a very long time (often many years on Broadway), it is harder and harder to get attention for a show, and publicists can get very desperate. Nobody said it was an easy job!

A publicist can't make people say nice things—but the publicist is always blamed for it if they don't!

Stage Notes

✳ As a publicity stunt, the cast of *Frozen* saluted the seventy-fifth anniversary of the classic Rodgers and Hammerstein musical *Oklahoma!* on March 31, 2018, with a curtain call sing-along of "Oh, What a Beautiful Mornin'" led by John Riddle. *Frozen* opened at the St. James Theatre, where *Oklahoma!* originally opened in 1943. It later played all over the Internet.

✳ Rather than a standard photo shoot on the theater stage, *Vanity Fair* photographers shot the cast of *Frozen*—Caissie Levy as Elsa, Patti Murin as Anna, and Jelani Alladin as Kristoff—against the snowcapped Rocky Mountains in Leadville, Colorado, during the out-of-town tryout in Denver.

✳ A one-time-only "guest star" is a popular way to promote a show. *Aladdin* has had cameo appearances by Natalie Morales, Al Roker, Whoopi Goldberg, and James Corden; Sherri Shepherd of *The View* guested in *Newsies*—and also flew as Mary Poppins (but only for the TV cameras).

✳ When veteran publicist Chris Boneau was in college and acting in a production of *Oedipus*, he looked out into the audience and realized that there were not enough people in the theater. He started to think about ways to attract more people to the show. He realized he must be a terrible actor because he was thinking about publicity when he should have been thinking about acting. He walked off the stage and went into the publicity business.

"There is only one thing in the world worse than being talked about, and that is not being talked about."

Oscar Wilde, from
The Picture of Dorian Gray

Tony Award winner Christopher Oram at work. "We're telling a story," he says. "It's always about telling a story."

DID YOU KNOW?

Set designer Christopher Oram says of his *Frozen* work, "The set is crammed full of references, homages, and 'Easter eggs' to all my favorite movies and other Broadway shows. It's kind of a proper treasure hunt. If you know where to look, it's all over the place."

SET DESIGNER

The **set designer**'s job is to take the audience on a visual journey by creating the world of the play. Everything on the stage except the actors and what they are wearing is a creation of the set designer. Sometimes stage sets and scenery are very literal, meaning that they look literally like real life. You might think, "Gosh, that looks just like a living room in a real house!" Other times the scenery is there to evoke a feeling about a place—or to suggest no place at all. It might just be a pile of dirt or blue carpeting across the floor and up the walls. These are all choices the set designer makes.

The designer's challenge is that they can't move the audience around, so they have to think about how to position the scenery to give the audience the best view. When you see a movie, the camera—the "point of view"—is always moving, but with a play the point of view doesn't change because you have to stay in your seat! The designer must make sure that each person gets the most impact possible from that one view.

The set designer also needs to think about what style of theater the set will be in. They design a very different set for a thrust stage than they do for an in-the-round or proscenium production.

Some plays are performed entirely with one set. Other plays have many sets that change during the performance. The designer not only has to figure out what is onstage, but also how it all fits backstage.

Sometimes scenery is designed to move behind the curtain, where you can't see how it is done. Other times it is moved by people or machines— or even sometimes by the actors right in front of you. These are all choices the designer and the director make to communicate what they want you to think and feel about the world they are creating.

The set designer and the lighting designer depend on each other a great deal. Without the lighting designer, no one would see the set. Lighting can also make the set look glorious or terrible. On the flip side, if there is no set, the lighting designer has very little to light.

Patti Murin, Kevin Del Aguila

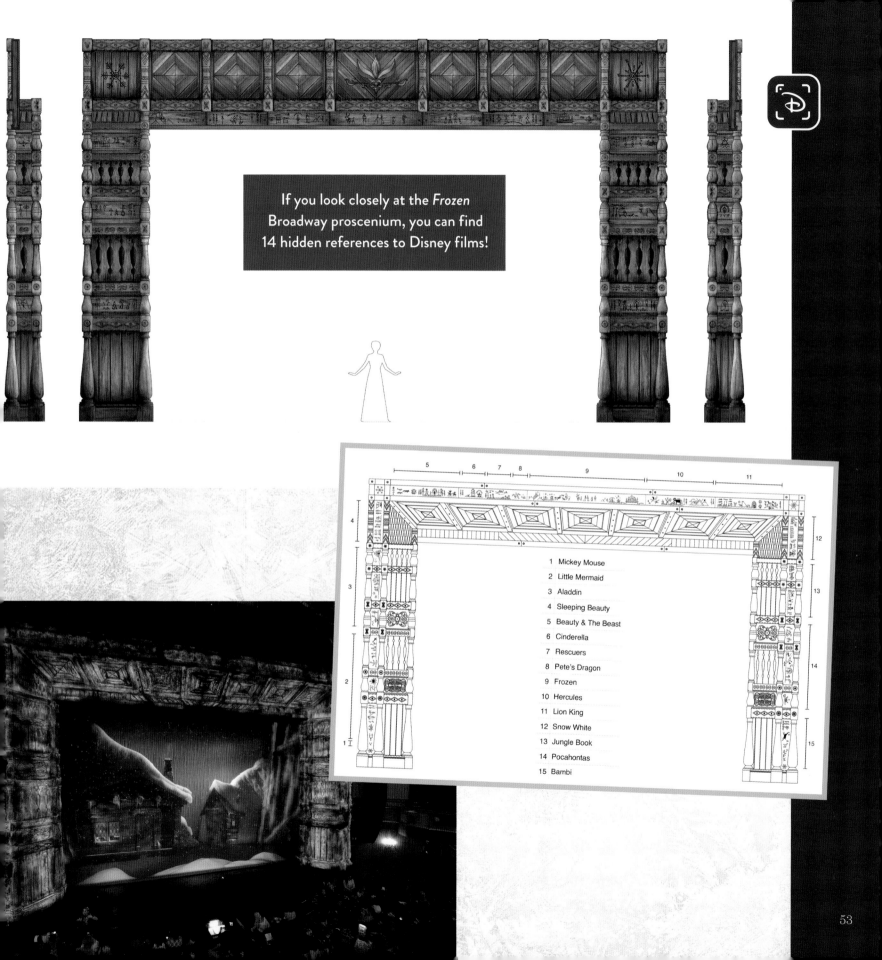

If you look closely at the *Frozen* Broadway proscenium, you can find 14 hidden references to Disney films!

1 Mickey Mouse
2 Little Mermaid
3 Aladdin
4 Sleeping Beauty
5 Beauty & The Beast
6 Cinderella
7 Rescuers
8 Pete's Dragon
9 Frozen
10 Hercules
11 Lion King
12 Snow White
13 Jungle Book
14 Pocahontas
15 Bambi

SET MODELS

Set models are like dollhouse versions of what will become the full set of a show. They are very valuable tools that help the designer show the producer, director, and choreographer what the show will look like, and how and where all the scenery will move. Set models help the director visualize where she will put the actors before the scenery is built, and they act as a guide for the people who will build the life-size set.

In rehearsal, actors only work with the barest elements of the set and don't see the completed one until it is installed in the theater. Models are sometimes the only way everyone can tell what a set will look like before it is built—and after it's built, you can't make changes!

Stage Notes

✳ In Shakespeare's time, there were no sets at all. The actors would suggest in their lines where they were. "Oh, my, this storm is blowing so hard I think this ship might sink" could be a line to suggest where the play was taking place. You wouldn't have to build a boat onstage at all. (Then again, the actor would have to say something a lot more interesting than just that dumb line if there were no scenery to look at all night.)

✳ Set designer Christopher Oram found a challenge in representing the relatively epic scale of *Frozen* within the proscenium. "We are in a relatively constricted space, and we have to take the audience from the girls' bedroom to the ballroom to the chapel to a garden and the courtyard—and that's even before we've left the castle," Oram says. The characters then go up a mountain and build an ice palace before heading to a general store and sauna.

✳ Everyone who works in the theater has stories about things that go wrong with scenery. When it is actually happening in front of the audience, it's terrible. But soon after, people can't wait to tell the story of how they cleverly survived the "disaster." Everyone tries to tell a story wilder than the one before it about these crazy nights.

> "The scenery in the play was beautiful, but the actors got in front of it."
>
> *Alexander Woollcott,*
> *critic and commentator*

FROZEN SET DESIGN PROGRESSION

Look at the set design from *Frozen* on Broadway as it goes from sketches to its appearance onstage!

 **1** Sketch

 **2** Model

3 Model "on Stage"

4 Final Set

SOUND DESIGNER

Theater has always had sound. When actors speak they make sound, a slamming door makes a sound, and an instrument makes a sound. In the theater, the person who makes sure you hear all those things is the **sound designer**. Sometimes they just make everything louder by playing it through a microphone, but sometimes they have to create the sound from scratch, like recording and playing back the sound of rain.

Once upon a time, everything you heard in a theater was created live by somebody. There were no microphones to make things louder or recorders to play back sound effects. Of course, once upon a time, there was no electricity for lights or heat to keep the theater warm—or even a good place to take a shower, to make it easy to sit next to the stranger who bought the ticket for the seat next to yours!

Theater is more fun today, if you ask me.

Frozen's sound designer Peter Hylenski, and the amazing Cassy Givens. She runs the board and "mixes" each show.

Today, sound designers have the complicated job of managing or creating all the sound you hear. In Broadway musicals, most actors wear tiny microphones to amplify their voices. The instruments in the orchestra are played into microphones, and the sound effects are all recorded. The sound designer figures out exactly what equipment to use and exactly where to place it so the sound is good in every seat in the theater. They also make sure that the sound is well-blended and balanced so that the audience hears everything just right.

Sound designers need to know a great deal about a lot of high-tech equipment. Their job is a lot harder than turning the stereo up or down. Sometimes there are more than sixty live microphones onstage and in the orchestra pit at one time! Each has to be balanced with the other, or you'll hear the third girl on the left instead of the leading lady during her big song—and trust me, the leading lady won't be happy about that!

They need to have very sensitive hearing to be able to make everything sound natural and like it's coming from the stage. They also need to be storytellers who know exactly what sound to play and when. What type of gunshot should be heard? Is that the sound of a lion or a jackal in the distance? What sort of birds live in that part of the country and would be singing outside the window?

SOUND OPERATOR

The sound designer plans all the sounds before the show happens, but the **sound operator** executes the sound designer's plan while the show is actually going on. The sound operator is often a different person from the sound designer, but in smaller productions the same person might do both jobs. The sound operator is in charge of the nightly running of the sound department, from distributing and testing the microphones and speakers, to controlling the volume of the sound heard during the performance. This job gets more and more difficult as the technology advances.

Watching a sound operator on a big Broadway musical is like watching a recording engineer mix music in a big recording studio. The operator also has to run all the prerecorded sound effects. And that's not easy. It takes a lot of hand-eye coordination to do it just right. If you are really good at video games, you might be a good sound operator, because both things take similar skills. For example, you might find yourself having to push a button at just the right time to make sure the audience hears the sound of a breaking plate just as an actor smashes a fake plate over someone's head!

Microphone

James Monroe Iglehart

Caissie Levy

Stage Notes

❋ The traditional place to wear a wireless microphone is on the forehead, as shown on Elsa above. In *Aladdin*, however, the Genie is played by a bald actor, so the microphone is tucked into his beard!

❋ When everyone onstage is wearing tiny wireless microphones, it is essential that the mics only be on when that person is talking or singing. If they are all left on at other times, each microphone will pick up random sounds onstage. Worse, if they are left on when the actors are backstage, just imagine what the audience would hear.

COSTUME DESIGN

A costume is everything the actor does (or does not) wear, and it is an important part of telling a story onstage.

The costume can range from a beautiful hand-beaded dress or shiny tuxedo to a complex bodysuit that makes an actor look like they aren't wearing any clothes at all, like Christopher Oram designed for the song "Hygge" in *Frozen*! A costume can include masks and stilts, as with Julie Taymor's giraffe costumes in *The Lion King*; or it can feature giant, gilded cutlery, like Ann Hould-Ward's forks and spoons in *Beauty and the Beast*. In *Aladdin*, costume designer Gregg Barnes designed a secret harness inside the costume, so the actors could attach themselves to the flying carpet! How the costume looks and how it moves onstage are decisions made by the costume designer to help tell the story at hand.

Theatrical costumes tell the audience about the characters they are watching: whether they are young or old, a boy or a girl, a doctor or a ditch digger, rich or poor, shy or wild.

For instance, if you see a girl in a long white gown with a veil and a bouquet of flowers, you'd probably guess she's a bride at her wedding, but if you see her in that same costume covered in mud, you can be sure something went wrong.

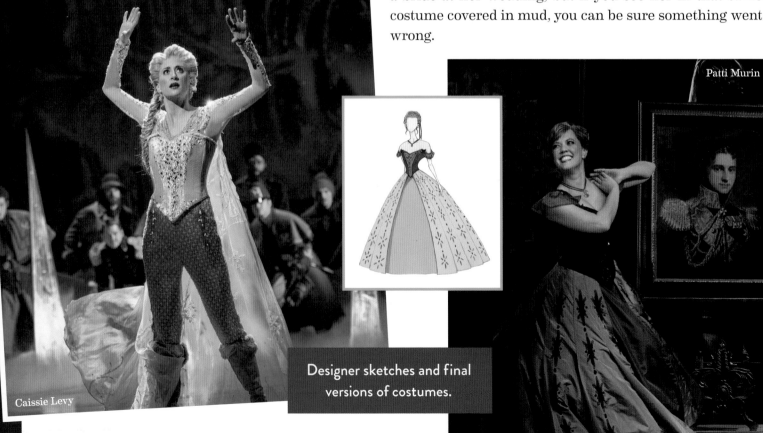

Designer sketches and final versions of costumes.

Patti Murin

Caissie Levy

Christopher Oram

Andrew Pirozzi; Jelani Alladin

Stage Notes

❋ Costumes are not just what you see onstage. Great designers also design the underwear and corsets for a character so that they will move and feel like someone who lived in that time period.

❋ A "quick change" is when an actor (usually) goes into the wings and has mere seconds to change their clothes before they come back onstage. There are many tricks to the process, including wearing one costume under the other, magnet fasteners that replace buttons, and lots of practice! Aladdin makes his quick change from pauper to Prince Ali in a few seconds, hidden by other actors. Elsa makes her quick change in full view of the audience all alone onstage!

❋ A swing actor (see page 88) in *The Lion King* who covers both dancing and singing roles needs over twenty different costumes to be able to do their job.

In twenty-four seconds, Aladdin changes clothes, onstage but hidden behind other actors, to become Prince Ali.

James Monroe Iglehart, Adam Jacobs

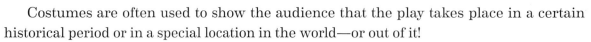

Costumes are often used to show the audience that the play takes place in a certain historical period or in a special location in the world—or out of it!

Costumes can even communicate the time of day or the weather. If you see someone in shorts, sunglasses, flip-flops, and a T-shirt, you might think it's summer and they are at the beach. A long fur coat means it's winter.

Sometimes, a costume designer creates clothing that they think the character would actually wear if they were a real person. Every detail can be created to look absolutely realistic and natural. On the other hand, theatrical costumes can be exaggerated or extravagant, creating a world of fantasy where the costume plays an important job in creating the visual wonder of a production.

Normally, the designer sketches the idea of what a character will look like, and a costume is built from scratch.

Sometimes the designer works with clothes from a large collection of costumes and "pulls" different items to mix and match into just the right look for a particular show. Like you would do if you had a *giant* closet at home. In the case of a production that is set in the present day, some costume designers will go to a variety of stores and "shop the show," buying just the right thing for each character. Before all those clothes you see in a show got onstage, the costume designer had to make the choices of design, color, fit, and movement to create the character.

Michael James Scott

Adam Jacobs, Courtney Reed

62

Everything someone wears or doesn't wear onstage is a *choice* the costume designer makes.

Costume designers are also responsible for making the clothes look "lived in" and the proper age. They will often add wrinkles and stains and sweat marks. They will sandpaper edges and tear at the fabric to make it look worn out.

Costume designers work very closely with makeup and hair and wig designers to create the complete "look" of a character.

Ryann Redmond

Mattea Conforti

63

HAIR AND WIGS

You may know an aunt, uncle, teacher, or librarian who wears a wig. Wigs are head coverings made of real or artificial hair. Sometimes it's hard to tell they're fake; other times it's so obvious that it's fun. In theater, a wig is often part of an actor's costume. Wigs can conveniently hide baldness or change the color of an actor's hair. An actress with a short hairstyle can instantly have long flowing locks, or an actor with a modern haircut can put on his hairpiece and step back in time.

The style of wigs and hairpieces can range from completely natural looking to larger-than-life and fantastic—depending on what's needed to tell the story and to communicate the character's identity.

Wig design involves two important skills: making the wig and styling it. A wig designer creates wigs for use onstage and also designs mustaches, beards, and sideburns. Wig designers build each hairpiece to fit the actor's exact head measurements, and they style the wigs before every performance.

Like costume design, hair and wigs support the story, and help visually identify the character, making their role clearer to an audience. A character's hairdo can say a lot about their personality and role.

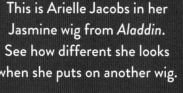

This is Arielle Jacobs in her Jasmine wig from *Aladdin*. See how different she looks when she puts on another wig.

Tyrell Martori, Caissie Levy

Stage Notes

❄ Most Broadway wigs are made out of real human hair. The hair is bought all over the world—some people in faraway countries grow their hair *just* to sell it to wig makers. They may live on a farm in the Czech Republic, or in India, but their hair is starring on Broadway eight performances a week!

❄ The strangest wigs *Frozen* designer David Brian Brown ever made were for a bunch of Broadway chorus girls who needed to have hairy armpits. He made little tiny wigs for them to put under their arms.

❄ Designer Josh Marquette created the hair for *Aladdin*. The Jasmine wig has extra-thick hair. It takes fifty hours to make one of her three wigs for the show. Her gorgeous wig with the ponytail with "bulbs" of hair is held together by a long piece of elastic that is pulled up once the bulbs are set. You could never make your real hair look like this!

❄ It is impossible to make a wig with short hair. A wig designer always begins working with long hair, and then cuts it to the right length—and that means they need a *lot* of hair!

Legendary hair designer David Brian Brown adjusts Caissie Levy as Elsa.

Frozen has sixty-seven wigs onstage every night, and everyone knows Elsa is *all* about her hair. She literally lets it down in "Let It Go" to symbolize that she's gone to a new place in her life. Elsa wears four wigs in the show. Each is very dense and heavy because the hair is so thick. Although you'd think her hair is white or platinum, there are actually *seven* different colors of hair blended together, strand by strand. And it takes twenty-four inches of hair to make her thick braid that she "lets go."

Anna's hair is part of her character, too. She has eight wigs (between the two actresses who play the character, young and grown-up) plus two hairpieces that get added on. Her hair needs to change color through the story as she gets more "frozen," and of course she needs some crazy "bed head" hair when the maids wake her up!

Chef Louis, *The Little Mermaid*

One actor can play many parts in many shows with the help of makeup, hair, and costume. Just like my friend Bobby Creighton.

Scuttle, *The Little Mermaid*

Timon, *The Lion King*

Weselton, *Frozen*

Watch Bobby begin his day by checking in at
the Stage Door of the St. James Theatre.

MAKEUP DESIGN

Everyone knows that actors wear makeup in the theater, but who decides what it looks like? All productions are different. For contemporary plays in modern dress, the actors and the costume designer or hair designer often sort it out and present the completed look to the director.

For a large but more traditional show like *Aladdin* or *Frozen*, the job of creating just the right look for an ice queen or a madcap and spirited genie is complicated but ultimately more conventional.

Get to know Cheryl Thomas, one of the makeup associates at *Aladdin*, here working on Michael James Scott.

A great deal of care goes into each design. The Genie in *Aladdin*, with makeup designed by Milagros Medina-Cerdeira, wears *three* colors of glitter on his face: gold, royal blue, and copper!

Some makeup is worn on the body. This is, logically, called body makeup. Body makeup takes a long time to put on and is almost impossible to use in a show with a lot of costume changes.

In *Frozen*, the characters known in the film as trolls are now based on mythic characters of Norway called the huldra. They have body makeup and specially designed transfer tattoos. (Many actors first have to cover their own tattoos with makeup and then put on the body markings for the character.) The "tattoos" were designed by costume designer Christopher Oram and are much like the temporary tattoos you can buy in shops and wear for fun.

In *The Lion King*, some actors change their face makeup more than a dozen times during the show. *The Lion King* has perhaps the most complicated makeup design in Broadway history. The designs that director and costume designer Julie Taymor oversaw with makeup designer Michael Ward are complex, gorgeous, and time-consuming. Some of the designs take a full hour to put on before *each* performance! Rafiki in *The Lion King* is painted with elaborate patterns that are filled in almost like an oil painting.

DID YOU KNOW?

You've heard of a costume change! But did you know there can also be makeup changes? In the middle of "Friend Like Me," the ensemble women change their costumes and their makeup—adding a gold shimmery eye shadow and a bright red lip color!

MAKEUP CREW

The makeup department re-creates the makeup designer's creations nightly. They also make sure all the actors who apply their own makeup are doing it correctly and have the supplies they need to get it done.

The makeup crew members are also the "makeup police," making sure that no one is putting on too much just to get extra attention, or too little to make cleaning up after the show easier.

The makeup crew helps actors in their dressing rooms, in the makeup room, or backstage in the dark between scenes. It is very common for makeup artists to hold small "bite-lites" in their mouths, pointed at an actor's face, while they quickly make adjustments or changes backstage.

The makeup crew requires specialized training, and most great makeup designers started working on a makeup crew.

Frozen makeup designer Anne Ford-Coates adjusts Caissie Levy's look.

69

Stage Notes

✳ Makeup artist Jorge Vargas (*Aida, Tarzan®, The Little Mermaid*) says that makeup is not always for the audience—some details can't be seen even in the first row. Actors might need to wear the "mask" of makeup to help them get into character or feel like someone else. For one Disney show, Jorge waited in the wings each night for one of the actresses to exit the stage, and he made a very small change to her makeup before she went back out for a very emotional scene. This little moment gave the actress a chance to focus on the change the character was experiencing.

✳ As stage lighting has improved over the past two decades, stage makeup has changed dramatically. The better the light, the less makeup the actors need to wear to distinguish their features.

✳ It is now very common for actors and actresses to have complex personal tattoos that usually are not appropriate for the character they are playing. Today it is typical for actors to arrive at the theater early to apply elaborate sweatproof makeup to cover tattoos that could otherwise be seen by the audience. Tattoos are a personal choice, but for the life of me I don't know why an actor wants to create a narrative on their body that will get in the way of the narrative they are playing onstage or on film.

Zhao Lei

Patti Murin, Gabbie Vincent

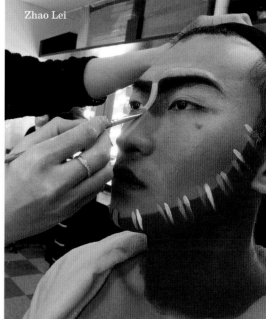

Zhao Lei

70

Broadway's Rafiki, Tshidi Manye, in full character makeup, designed by Michael Ward. The makeup takes almost a full hour to apply for every performance.

On with the Show

Now that you've found your seat and met some of the people who work on what you'll see, it's time to get ready for the show!

THEATER ETIQUETTE

Etiquette may be a fancy way of saying "the way you are supposed to behave," but it is essential to enjoying the theater for EVERYONE. Some people think they don't need to behave at all anymore—and for the life of me I don't understand what they are thinking.

Etiquette helps everyone get along, especially in crowded spaces. It should be obvious: don't talk like you are watching TV with your family at home, don't eat a meal, don't make noise with the ice in your drink, don't text on your phone, and don't take photos. Doesn't that sound easy?

For pity's sake, sit and watch the show with respect for others around you—or just stay home. No one wants to sit next to you if you are being rude, and no matter what you paid for your ticket, you did not pay for the right to ruin it for others. The theater is a temple of the arts. And no one has the right to ruin the experience for others, no matter where they are sitting.

And by the way: *don't bring a child that is not of an age to sit quietly and not disturb others*. Family shows are not day care!

What have we left out? What rude things do people do in the theater that bug you? Feel free to start your own list and share it with others!

> "The theatre should be treated with respect. The theatre is a wonderful place, a house of strange enchantment, a temple of illusion."
>
> *Noël Coward*

NO FOOD IN THE THEATER

NO TALKING IN THE THEATER

NO PHOTOGRAPHY, PLEASE

LEAVE YOUR BIG HAT AT HOME

The Play's the Thing

There are many kinds of shows. There are dramas set in historical times with large casts, and there are one-person plays. There are comedies set in the present day, and comedies that were written many, many years ago. There are musical comedies with loads of dancing and funny characters, and there are musicals that aren't funny at all. Some of the most popular musicals of all time don't have a laugh in them (unless someone falls down or breaks a prop by accident). Sometimes a show isn't a play or a musical, but a collection of songs that, when sung in a particular order, make sense in some way or mean something. For example, a collection of patriotic songs all sung together might make you feel good about the country you live in, or a bunch of romantic songs might make you feel romantic; or a bunch of songs about food might make you feel hungry— get the picture? That's normally called a revue. It can be hard to always put everything into a particular category, and that's probably a good thing. Not all ideas for shows fit neatly into the definitions set by what has come before. People are like that, too.

The following are some of the basic types of shows, so you'll know what people are talking about when you hear them.

DRAMA
Drama can mean a lot of things. "Oh, please, cut the drama" means stop overacting in life and just get on with it. Drama is also the universal art form of theater. Normally when we say a play is a drama, we mean that it is serious in nature and probably doesn't have a lot of laughs.

Our London production of *Shakespeare in Love* (above); Our production of *Peter and the Starcatcher* (below).

Lucy Briggs-Owen, Tom Bateman

Teddy Bergman, Christian Borle

73

COMEDY

Comedies are funny. They make you laugh—or hopefully at least smile. A really, really funny play is clearly a comedy. Some older plays are called comedies when the topic isn't too serious, but frankly they aren't all that funny and you shouldn't expect to get a stomachache from laughing all night. Sometimes plays that are just lighter in tone are called comedies, too.

MUSICAL

Musicals are plays that use music to tell the story and generally (but not always) mix up the songs with spoken words. *Beauty and the Beast* is a musical. So is *The Lion King*. Some people make the distinction between musical comedies and other types of musicals; some musicals aren't funny at all. *The Phantom of the Opera* doesn't have a lot of laughs, but people love it. The key element of musicals is that they tell their stories in song.

Elsa's coronation in *Frozen.*

CLASSIC

A classic is a play that was first performed long ago and still feels relevant today. To call something a classic is to give it credit for enduring because of its timeless meaning. The plays of Shakespeare are called classics because, although they were written more than five hundred years ago, we still find relevance and truth in their stories. The same is true about great older plays from many countries that have been translated into languages for audiences all over the world. A classic can be a drama or a comedy. Some theater companies dedicate themselves to producing only classic plays, and they do them in all styles, including performing classic plays in costumes that look just like the clothes we wear today.

REVIVAL

A revival is a play or musical that is being done after the first production has run and closed. A revival is generally done by different people from the ones who did it the first time, and most often runs many years later. A revival can look completely different from the original, or it can look sort of the same.

WATCHING THE PLAY

There are a few tricks to watching a play.

If it is a classic, try to read it, or read something about it, before you go. Sometimes the words can be hard to understand. The more you know beforehand, the easier it will be.

Use all of your senses. Listen, look, absorb it with every part of you. Allow yourself to be transported.

Most importantly, go in with an open mind. There's an old expression that applies to everything artistic: "You don't know what you like, you like what you know." It means you don't have a clue what you will like until you get to know it. The mind is like an umbrella—it won't work unless it's open! Keep that in mind every time you go to the theater.

OVERTURE

Some musicals start with a medley of the music you are about to hear, called an overture. It signals to the audience that it is time to pay attention (and stop talking, for pity's sake!), and hear some of the tunes that will be played during the evening. Not all musicals have overtures, but some of the best music ever written for the theater is in overtures. (At the start of act two there is often a miniature version of an overture. It's called the entr'acte. That's French for "hurry up and sit down, act two is starting.")

When the houselights go down and the curtain (if there is one) opens, it is one of the most exciting moments in the theater. The show is starting—and anything is possible. Enjoy!

INTERMISSION

Plays and musicals are broken into segments called acts. Most, but not all, musicals are broken into two acts. Plays are often in two acts, and some older ones are in three acts. Between the acts is a time to get a drink or stretch your legs. That break is called the intermission. In England, it's called the interval. If you are seeing a play with just one act, the program usually indicates that the show is presented "without an intermission." That's why I make it a habit to always visit the bathroom before the show starts. No one will ever give you better advice in life than that!

CURTAIN TIME

"Curtain time" is the time when the show starts. "What time is curtain?" means "What time does it start?" "Keeping the curtain up" means keeping the show going—even when things are going wrong—and "final curtain" means the time the show is over.

Newsies!

CENTER STAGE

Original Broadway production of *Frozen*.

Act II of *The Lion King* begins!

ACT TWO Back of House:
From the Stage Apron to the Stage Door

What's It Like to Be Up Onstage?

A stage is a very large platform with some areas that can be seen by the audience and other areas that can't be seen by the audience. **Onstage** means standing where the audience is able to see you. **Offstage** usually means outside of view of the audience but still on the actual stage. The area called the wings is offstage. For example, you might ask an actor to wait "just offstage" and then run on when they hear a gunshot. Backstage means all the areas out of the view of the audience, but especially the area where all the preparation happens. Backstage is the general term for any place the audience doesn't go. That can mean wardrobe rooms, carpentry shops, wig rooms, or even just offstage in the wings.

UP, DOWN, LEFT, RIGHT—WHEN I'M ONSTAGE, WHERE AM I?

The stage is divided up into areas like a map. Do you know how to find north, south, east, and west? Well, a stage is divided like that, too. You absolutely have to know these directions like the back of your hand to work in the theater!

- If you stand in the center of the stage, you are standing **center stage**.

- If you are standing center stage and facing the audience, you are facing **downstage**.

- If you are standing center stage and facing downstage, the area behind you is **upstage**.

- If you are standing center stage facing the audience with your back to upstage, you will find **stage right** on your own right and **stage left** on your left.

TO REVIEW
Center is in the middle. **Downstage** is toward the audience. **Upstage** is away from the audience. **Right** is to your right, and **left** is to your left when you face the audience.

DON'T THEY KNOW UP FROM DOWN?
Why is the upstage up and the downstage down? A long time ago (and even sometimes today), stages were sloped toward the audience, with the higher part away from the audience and the lower part towards the audience. This helped the audience see everything onstage. That slope is called a **rake**. When you hear "Is the stage raked?" it means "Does it slope?" Once you know that, and think about it for a minute (I'll wait), it is easy to understand why it is called **upstage** and **downstage**. The names of other parts of the stage are pretty obvious, aren't they?

TRAPPED!
There is one more location on the stage, and that goes straight down below the floor—through a **trap**. A trap is a hole in the floor that you can enter the stage from, exit through, or bring scenery or props through. There are many different kinds of trapdoors, and some stages have many of them; they can be very useful ways to create simple stage illusions or bring up entire rooms full of scenery. Some traps have lifts in them—they appear to magically lift the actor or scenery onto the stage or make them disappear through the floor.

TEST YOURSELF!
Take a piece of paper and mark one of the long sides with a D at the edge. The piece of paper is now your stage. The D is the audience edge of the stage, or downstage. Now put a U on the opposite edge. That's upstage. You can now figure out where to put the R for right, L for left, and C for center.

Mark where you think downstage right is. The director would say to an actor, "Now, I want you to walk downstage right when you say that line," and you know that would be toward the audience, but also towards the right. Right?

Where is upstage left? Left of center? Where would you be going? The basic upstage, downstage, stage right, and stage left positions can be used in lots of combinations. It's like a code.

NOW TRY THIS
Find a place without a lot of stuff in the way, like an empty garage or a playground. Pretend it's a stage and decide where the wings are. Ask a friend (or more than one) to stand center stage, facing downstage. You stand where the audience would be and start giving stage directions.

If you want your friends to go to your left, you need to tell them to go stage right, because your left is their right when you face each other. The directions are always from the actor's side, and the director has to think backward. Give lots of directions: go upstage center, stand downstage left, enter upstage left and walk (or cross, as we say in the theater) to downstage right. Switch roles and let your friend be the director and you be the actor. Can you keep your directions straight?

Enrico del Pieri, Richard-Salvador Wolff

How Can You Get Onstage—and Then What Happens?

CASTING

There are many elements in a show that need to be just right, or the show won't work. Casting is one of them. It isn't just about getting good actors. It's about getting an actor who's good for a particular role. Some of the best actors in the world are just not right for certain parts, and casting the right people is the job of the producer, the director of the play, and the casting director. The casting director is responsible for finding and bringing in potential actors for every role so that the producer and director can decide who can play what character.

Another tricky part of casting is that on a long-running show like *The Lion King* or *Beauty and the Beast*, you can't expect the original cast to stay with the show for years and years. That means that actors in all the parts—big or small—are always coming and going. Casting isn't just about who's onstage opening night. It's about who's onstage as long as the show is playing. So, what does the actor have to do to land a part?

Casting director Bernie Telsey (left); casting director Tara Rubin with *On The Record* director Bobby Longbottom (right).

AUDITION

Auditions are when actors perform in some way for the creative team of the show to demonstrate that they are right for a certain part. All auditions are different, and because auditioning is so important (it's how you get the job, after all), there are whole books written about how to do it well.

For a musical, an audition usually requires singing, dancing, and acting. The director knows what she is looking for and structures an audition process that will help her find the best actors for that particular show. For example, when casting a show like *Tarzan*® with a lot of apes onstage, she might ask actors to show that they can move around like a gorilla and walk on their knuckles or flip backward. Actors need to be ready for anything!

Most actors who work on musicals always carry a bag with them that has sheet music for several songs in different styles that represent how they sing.

If the director wants a love ballad, the prepared actor has one ready to go. If the director wants a fast song with a rock beat, they have that, too. The same goes for shoes and clothes. *Want to see me tap-dance? I've got tap shoes. Want jazz or ballroom dancing? I've got shoes in here for that, too.* If the show has a special requirement, like roller-skating, the actors are told that ahead of time so they can prepare.

Before auditioning for a play, actors are usually given a scene or two by the casting director—or whoever is in charge of the casting process—to prepare on their own and read in front of the director and producer. Sometimes during the audition, the director will suddenly ask an actor to read for the part of a character they were not called in to play or to read an unfamiliar scene. Again, the actor must be ready for anything.

Auditions test many things about actors. Of course they show how well actors can perform, but they also reveal how well they can adapt to change or direction.

Auditions also teach the show's creators about their show. Sometimes it is the first time they will have seen any of the choreography or the first time they've heard someone other than the composer sing the songs. When

Tony Award–winning actor Shuler Hensley auditioned for the role of Kerchak in *Tarzan*®, he was a different type of actor than what the director was looking for. He didn't fit the character description that had been sent out, but the casting director, Bernie Telsey, knew he was a brilliant actor and singer. Shuler "reinvented" the character in front of the show's creators and was cast in the role. Because of his audition and interpretation of the character, new scenes and even a new song were added to the script, and the show will forever be better for it.

CALLBACKS

Once the actors are done auditioning, they must go home and wait for a callback. Callbacks are when actors audition a second (or third or fourth) time after the first audition. Usually many people audition, and as callbacks proceed, the selection gets smaller and smaller as you get closer to casting the show. At callbacks, actors may be asked to do the same thing again, or to play scenes with other actors who are also auditioning to see how they look together.

REHEARSAL

Once the cast is picked, it's time to get to work! The rehearsal process for every show is different, but no matter what the show is or who is in it, the rehearsals are the process of learning the script and learning what to do onstage. The director tries all of his ideas, and the actors try as many of their ideas as the director will let them. Rehearsals for musicals are a bit different from those for other plays because musicals need music and choreography. Most musicals rehearse in several rooms simultaneously—some actors practice the songs while others work on scenes onstage, for example—to learn all the different aspects of the production. Straight plays usually rehearse in one space. No matter how the rehearsals are done, by the end of the process the show should be ready to perform.

Rehearsals can be joyful or agonizing, and often are both. It is a time when everyone learns about each other and about the show. Behaving well in rehearsals when everything is constantly changing, lines and songs are being cut, and dances are being learned, undone, and relearned is a very important part of working in the theater. If you don't like rehearsing, the theater probably isn't for you.

> "To achieve great things, two things are needed: a plan and not quite enough time."
>
> —Leonard Bernstein

Original Young Annas and Elsas for Broadway: Mattea Conforti, Ayla Schwartz, Audrey Bennett, and Brooklyn Nelson.

BLOCKING

Blocking is the process of telling the actor where to move and what to do. The director "blocks," or stages, the show, the actor learns the blocking by doing it and writing it in his script, and the stage manager records the blocking in her script so she knows exactly where everyone is and how they got there. Blocking is very important. If you're lucky and the show is a hit, you'll have to teach the blocking to many other actors who will play that part.

LOAD-IN

While the actors are in the rehearsal room learning the show, the technical crew is loading in the scenery and lights. Load-in can be a simple process, like loading in a piano and a couple of stools, or it can take a couple of months for a large Broadway show such as *The Lion King*. Compared with loading in permanent sets, as on Broadway, touring shows are designed (and rehearsed) to load in very quickly—sometimes even in eight hours. Ideally all the scenery and lighting will be in place and operating perfectly before the actors arrive.

I've never seen that happen. Not once.

DRY TECH

Dry tech is a technical rehearsal where all the scene changes and lighting cues are sorted out and practiced before the actors get onstage. It is a very useful process—in fact, it is an essential one.

It can be great fun during the dry tech to see a large piece of scenery move perfectly and gracefully on cue for the very first time. It is a lot less fun in dry tech to watch that massive piece of scenery crash into another large piece of scenery right before your very eyes. The only thing you can be happy about is that the actors weren't there to see it, too!

TECHNICAL REHEARSALS

These kinds of rehearsals can be long and slow and painstaking, as the entire cast and crew goes from the top of the show and rehearses every light cue, every scene change, every entrance, every moment of flying or stage magic, with all the elements in place. This is where your nerves are tested. There is never enough time, everyone is anxious over whether or not the show is going to work, all usually seems lost, the hours are very long, nothing is working, and you wonder why you aren't working at a bank instead.

One of the most difficult technical rehearsals ever for a Broadway show had to be *The Lion King*. The show is massive, and there are so many costumes and puppets and masks to be organized and so much scenery to move around that it would drive anyone crazy. Very late one night, when the cast and crew had been rehearsing for many weeks and everyone was at their wits' end, Heather Headley, who was playing the lioness Nala, quietly began singing the song "Summertime" from the legendary musical *Porgy and Bess*. At first she just sang quietly to herself as she waited for a lighting cue to be sorted. People began to hear it, and all over the theater they stopped what they were doing and became quiet. No one said a word. Everyone just knew they were hearing something special from an actress who was destined for greatness. In that silent theater, her voice filled the space and reminded everyone why they loved the theater and why they were working so hard. When she finished, everyone erupted into applause and the technical rehearsals for that show changed—they became just a little easier.

By the end of technical rehearsals, the show should be able to go from first curtain up to final curtain without stopping. I've never seen it go that well, but that's what is supposed to happen!

The theater looks a lot different when we're at work on a show.

DRESS REHEARSAL

Dress rehearsals are when the actors perform the show in full costumes, wigs, and makeup on the set with all the lighting, props, and scenery just as they will be when the audience gets to see it. Often there are many dress rehearsals. The first one can be a total disaster as you try to put all the pieces together and learn what doesn't work.

Everything feels different at dress rehearsal: the wig causes an actress to get confused, the costume change is too slow between scenes, the actor didn't realize he wouldn't be able to put his arm around the actress because her dress is so gigantic he can't even reach her. . . .

You get the picture.

Performers

There are lots of categories of performers onstage, and there are different names for them. Whether male or female, singer, dancer, acrobat, or aerialist, everyone onstage is there to tell the story and make the audience believe, for just an hour or two, that there is a world on that stage that is worth paying attention to.

Everyone onstage is telling the story, and so to me, they are all actors. But here are the technical differences.

PRINCIPAL ACTOR

The principal actors play the main roles. They can also be called the leading actors. Some big roles are also referred to as "featured actor," meaning that it is a big part, but not quite as big as the leading actor. Some actors like to count the lines their character says in the show. Or count the songs. Some actors worry that the part isn't big enough. All they should really worry about is whether they are any good or not.

ENSEMBLE ACTOR

In a musical, ensemble actors play many smaller roles and appear in the larger musical numbers. Once upon a time, the ensemble was referred to as the "chorus" and was separated into singers and dancers. Today, ensemble actors are expected to do both. Sometimes, a director will cast a brilliant dancer and ignore her singing, or cast an amazing singer and ignore his dancing, but they have to be really amazing in their specialty. Most ensemble actors need to be strong in both skills.

Also, many members of the ensemble cover, or understudy, the leading roles (more on that later). That second girl from the right in a production number just might be playing the lead role tomorrow night!

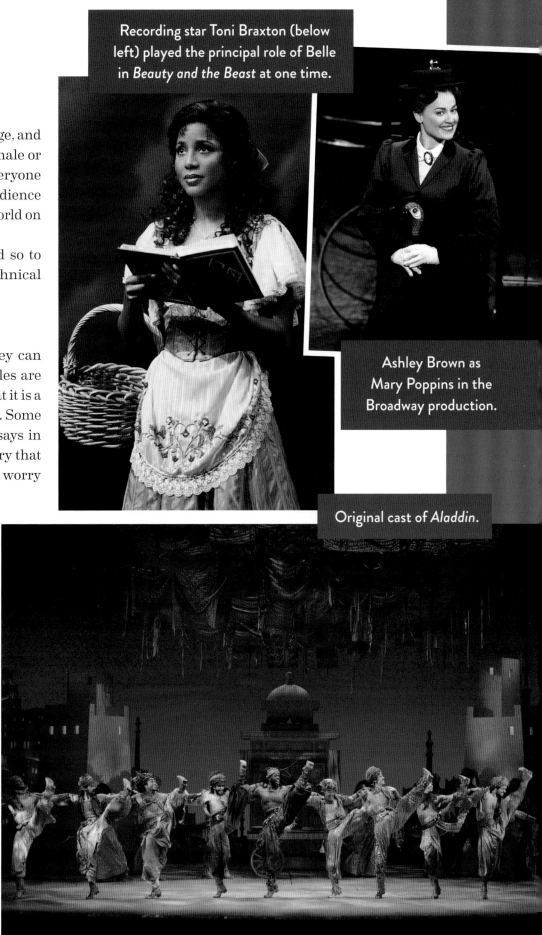

Recording star Toni Braxton (below left) played the principal role of Belle in *Beauty and the Beast* at one time.

Ashley Brown as Mary Poppins in the Broadway production.

Original cast of *Aladdin*.

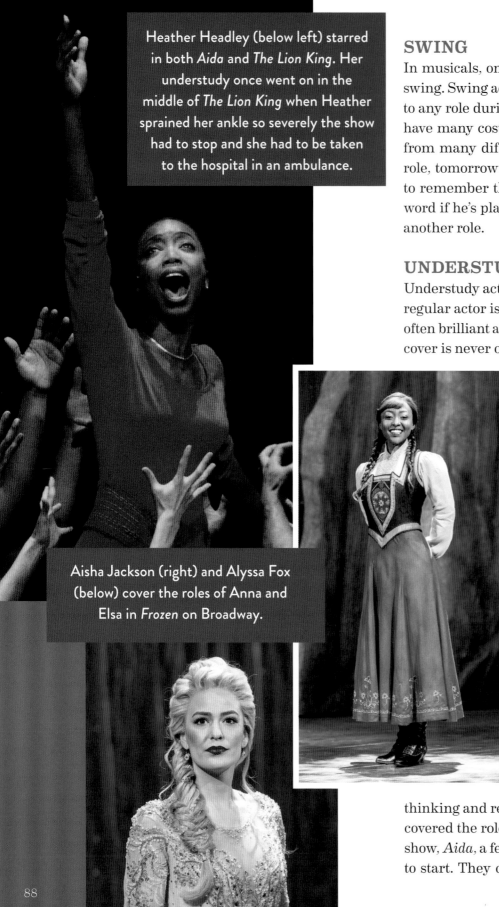

Heather Headley (below left) starred in both *Aida* and *The Lion King*. Her understudy once went on in the middle of *The Lion King* when Heather sprained her ankle so severely the show had to stop and she had to be taken to the hospital in an ambulance.

Aisha Jackson (right) and Alyssa Fox (below) cover the roles of Anna and Elsa in *Frozen* on Broadway.

SWING

In musicals, one of the most exciting and challenging roles is the swing. Swing actors are called this because they can just "swing in" to any role during the dance and production numbers. The swings have many costumes, and they learn the choreography and songs from many different positions. Tonight a swing might be in one role, tomorrow another. He has to watch the show very carefully to remember that in the big number he turns right on a certain word if he's playing one part, but left on the same word if he plays another role.

UNDERSTUDY

Understudy actors (or cover actors) play the leading roles when the regular actor is sick, on vacation, or unavailable. Understudies are often brilliant actors who never get to go on, because the person they cover is never out. Other times, they go on all the time. Sometimes it's a big break for an understudy to go on, and everyone is watching from the wings to see how they will do. I love to see understudies go on. It gives the show a fresh energy—and sometimes creates real panic backstage.

One night in *The Lion King* on Broadway, the actor playing the main character, Simba, was sick and couldn't perform. His understudy was sick, too, so he couldn't perform, either. There is always a second understudy on a big show, but in this case that guy had just joined the show. This was going to be his first night in the role. Well, the adult Simba first enters the stage by swinging from a rope—sort of like a rope swing that hangs from a tree. Thirty minutes before the show was to start, Simba raced onstage to rehearse this move for the first time. Something went wrong and he sprained his ankle—now he couldn't perform, either. The audience was out front taking their seats, and there was no one backstage who could play the part!

One of the stage managers did some quick thinking and realized that an original *Lion King* cast member who covered the role of Simba, was now performing in another Disney show, *Aida*, a few blocks away. It was now almost time for the show to start. They called over to *Aida* and the former *Lion King* actor was already in his costume and makeup, just about ready for the opening number of *Aida*. Well, Simba doesn't enter until the end of act one, so they rushed him to the *Lion King* theater five blocks away, his own understudy went on for *Aida*, and he got out of his *Aida* makeup and costume and changed into his *Lion King* makeup and costume and made it onstage just in time for his first entrance. He had not played the role of Simba in almost two years, and there he was in front of an audience that never knew anything had gone wrong!

Wendi Bergamini and Ross Lekites rehearse new choreography for *Frozen*.

A Day in the Life of a Child Performer

BY MATTEA CONFORTI

When you hear about "Broadway child actors," you may assume that we are all the same; that we all are homeschooled, or that we all live in New York City. Well, I am a child actor working on Broadway, but my life outside of the theater is very different from what you may be thinking. I do not live in New York City, and I am not homeschooled. I attend a public school in New Jersey, and most of my friends have nothing to do with show business at all. Some of my friends I have known since before I began acting professionally, and others I have met along the way. But to them, I am just Mattea, their crazy and fun-loving friend, who also happens to be on Broadway.

My typical day starts with a full day of school and then driving to New York City to the theater. I attend school every day except Wednesdays, when I go to a few morning classes but then leave early to make my matinee call time. When I miss school, I am tutored at the theater by my on-set teacher. It can be hard to miss school at times, but I try really hard—with the help of my parents and teachers—to stay organized and to keep an open line of communication with my school so that I can keep up with my assignments.

Once I am at the theater, I meet my guardian at the stage door, and I don't see my parents again until I come out after the show. Many people think that I have a parent backstage with me, or that either my mom or dad watches the show nightly, but that's not the case. Broadway kids are assigned guardians who are responsible for them during both rehearsals and performances. Our guardians make sure that we are happy, healthy, and safe at all times. You really develop a close relationship with your guardian. Mine has become like a big sister to me.

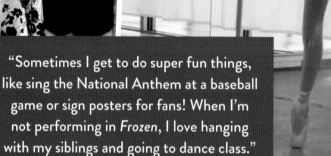

"Sometimes I get to do super fun things, like sing the National Anthem at a baseball game or sign posters for fans! When I'm not performing in *Frozen*, I love hanging with my siblings and going to dance class."

A Broadway child actor is also very lucky to develop close friendships with the people at their show. I have gotten very close to all the cast members, stage managers, crew, hair and makeup artists, dressers, security guards, and security dogs! The other *Frozen* girls are my "sisters," and I share a very special bond with them. When we are not doing our homework backstage, we play games together, do crafts, hang out—basically anything typical kids do to have fun.

Outside of the theater, I love to dance, sing, read, work out, play with my puppy, and play field hockey. I have been dancing since I was three years old, and before I got involved in acting, I was a competitive dancer. I still love to go to my dance school in New Jersey for lessons. In between shows on two-show days, I like to take dance or voice lessons with my New York–based teachers. I also love to spend my breaks with the other girls in the show. We try to take advantage of all New York City has to offer. Some of the things we like to do are get dinner at our favorite restaurants, have a picnic and play games in Bryant Park, and go to a movie, bowling, or to a museum.

I think it is very important for people to know that although working on Broadway is a lot of fun, it is also a lot of work, and it takes a lot of dedication, sacrifice, and support from family and friends to make it happen. I am so grateful that I have a very supportive family who have helped me achieve my dreams. I am especially grateful to my parents, grandparents, brother, and sister, who always support me no matter what, and who are an integral part of my journey.

Backstage

Only the performers and crew are allowed in the backstage area. So if someone from the show says to you, "Would you like to go backstage?" always say, "YES!" The show seen by the audience is no match for what happens "behind the scenes." All the areas behind the curtains, on the stage, and in the halls, or just places that are tented off from public view, are referred to as backstage, even if these areas are not actually anywhere near the stage itself.

The mystery of backstage, of course, is that it's where the magic is created. It's where actors can be seen in costume but not in character. "In character" means acting like the character and not themselves. In the performance you may see a sweet old lady who can barely stand, but backstage when no one is watching, that sweet old lady might be a beautiful young woman standing up straight and joking with her friends. The wig and costume and padding and cane may all be part of her costume, but backstage, before she is in character, she isn't an old lady at all.

Stage managers, actors, crew, orchestra members, theater management, and other people who work on the show freely walk around backstage and see the show from a very different point of view. Sometimes the young lovers onstage can't stand the sight of each other when they are backstage, and other times the characters who fight like cats and dogs onstage might just be the best of friends when you see them backstage. You never know!

Gigantic giraffe puppets used during the song "I Just Can't Wait to Be King" are stored backstage at *The Lion King*.

IF YOU HAD WINGS!

The sides of the stage, where actors stand hidden by curtains or scenery before they enter, are called the wings.

Wings are where some of the scenery is kept while it isn't onstage. Actors also stand in the wings before they enter or just after they have exited the stage. The wings can be dangerous because they are dark and scenery can come offstage very fast between scenes. If you are in the wrong place, you might just get run over by a castle, or a herd of wildebeests, or a bunch of chimney sweeps! Also, you have to be careful not to make noise that will distract the actors onstage or be heard by the audience out front.

The famous expression that someone is "waiting in the wings" literally means she is ready to go onstage. In real life, it can mean the person is waiting for her chance to be selected, or to do a job, or to be the center of attention. "She's waiting in the wings to become class president—just as soon as that obnoxious boy who's class president now moves out of town and gets out of our way!" Or something like that.

Tiny microphones (below) are laid out backstage with each character's name on them.

"It's Curtains for You, Mister!"

Cheesy gangster movie characters say that when they are about to kill somebody. It means, of course, that it's the end for someone. Well, the same is true in the theater—sort of. When the curtain goes up, it means things are starting, and when the curtain goes down, the show ends. But nobody gets killed!

There are as many different kinds of stage curtains as you can count on your fingers and toes—and your best friend's fingers and toes. There are curtains that separate the audience from the stage, there are curtains that block your view into the wings, there are curtains that are painted, there are curtains that are made of velvet, there are curtains that are designed so that you can see through them when the lights are adjusted in a certain way. Of course, not all theaters have curtains—but when you need them, they come in handy. Let's review the important ones.

MASKING CURTAINS

Masking is the most important job of curtains. Just like when you wear a Halloween mask so no one can see your face, curtains in the theater cover things that we don't want the audience to see.

There are two main kinds of masking curtains, called legs and borders. Legs are the narrow curtains that "stand up" on the sides—a lot like your legs. Borders are the ones that hang sideways on the top. These special curtains hide lighting instruments and other things hanging above the stage, and also prevent you from seeing actors in the wings.

This "painted backdrop" is actually a giant video screen for *Frozen*.

FRONT CURTAIN

The first curtain you are likely to see in a theater is the one that separates the audience from the stage. It hangs just upstage of the proscenium and has many names: show curtain, front cloth, main rag, act curtain, and house curtain.

There are two basic types of front curtains. The first kind go up and down, closing off the stage just like the blinds that raise and lower on your windows at home.

The other kind splits in the middle and opens side to side. These are like the fabric drapes that people sometimes hang over their windows instead of blinds.

BACKDROP

A backdrop is a piece of fabric that is stretched so tight that it looks like a solid wall. It hangs from a sideways pipe that can be raised or lowered. It is one of the most common forms of theatrical scenery. A backdrop can be painted to look like a forest or a city street or the inside of someone's house. Skilled painters can make them look three-dimensional and not flat at all.

Adam Jacobs

STAR DROP

One of the simplest and most beautiful draperies onstage is the star drop. This is a large black or dark blue velvet curtain with tiny little lights (like white Christmas lights) pulled through it from the back. The wires are all hidden, so all you see are pinpoints of light in a field of darkness. It can look just like stars on a clear night.

You can see star drops in many shows. In *The Lion King*, the lion Mufasa makes a speech to his son, Simba, where he tells him to look at the stars. Onstage, Mufasa sings a song about the meaning of the stars while the stars gently appear on a star drop hanging behind him.

Star drop in *Aladdin*.

Yukihiro Shimamura, Mizue Okamoto

SCRIM

A scrim is one of the most interesting curtains of all. It is made out of a special fabric; when lit from the front it looks like a normal painted backdrop, but when you light up what's behind it you can see right through it! Scrims can be one plain color or have a full scene painted on them. In *Mary Poppins*, we have a scrim that is painted to look like the outside of a house. When you light the scenery behind the scrim, the house disappears, and you look right through it.

SAFETY CURTAIN

The safety curtain doesn't have anything to do with the way the show looks. In fact, you hope the audience will never see it.

The safety curtain, sometimes called the fire curtain, is a fireproof curtain that closes off the stage area from the audience. Because theaters used to be very flammable, lawmakers decided that every theater should be required to have a fireproof curtain. If a fire were to break out onstage, this curtain would come down very quickly to keep the fire from going into the auditorium.

Fire has always been a big danger onstage. At one time, stage lights were gas-fueled flames, sort of like the lanterns you may use when you go camping. The scenery is frequently made of wood and other flammable materials. When you add to that the need for torches or candles in some scenes, everyone in the theater knows to be very careful with fire and fire safety.

CYCLORAMA

The cyclorama, or "cyc," is usually the farthest upstage curtain. Normally it covers the entire back wall, and unlike other draperies or backdrops it's usually completely blank. It is light-colored fabric and can be lit to look like the sky or just a beautiful color. The cyclorama is sometimes used to make the theater look like it's much deeper than it really is, because with just colored light on a vast expanse of fabric, you don't have any specific image to focus on to tell how far away it is.

Naidjun Severina, Steve Beirnaert, Kobe van Herwegen

The Rooms Backstage

There are many different areas backstage where the actors and crew prepare for the performance. Every theater is different, and many of them are cramped and old—not to mention drafty and badly heated, or full of bugs and rodents. Sounds glamorous, no? These are some of the spaces you'll find.

THE GREENROOM

The greenroom is where everyone gathers before going onstage. It's like a lounge or hangout. Very few Broadway theaters have greenrooms. Space backstage in these old buildings is precious, and more important things always seem to occupy that space. But greenrooms often exist in new theaters.

The origin of the term *greenroom* is unknown, and theater people all make up crazy stories to explain it when asked. But the best answer would be "I have no idea," because no one does!

The most widely accepted origin of the term dates back to Shakespearean theater. Actors would prepare for their performances in a room filled with plants and shrubs. It was believed that the moisture in the plants was beneficial to the actors' voices.

DRESSING ROOMS

Dressing rooms are designed for just that—dressing. Actors either have their own rooms, or share them with others. Generally, the wardrobe department delivers a costume to the dressing room each night, and actors prepare for the show there by warming up and putting on their makeup, wigs, and costumes. "Star" dressing rooms range from glamorous to little hole-in-the-wall spaces. Sometimes chorus members all share one big room. Great actors know how to make the best of these small spaces. Many years ago a well-known actor named Yul Brynner had become famous playing the king in the musical *The King and I* on Broadway. He demanded his dressing room be painted a specific color of brown. He later toured America in this role, and every theater he went to had to paint the star's dressing room "Brynner brown." Some of those dressing rooms stayed that color for many, many years, and other actors from then on knew they were sharing a dressing room with Yul Brynner!

Courtney Reed and Adam Jacobs meet people at the stage door after a performance of *Aladdin*.

STAGE DOOR

The stage door is where the cast, the crew, and anyone who works backstage enters the theater. They never come through the front door with the public. Traditionally, you will find three very important elements at the stage door.

The first is the stage doorman. On Broadway there is a long tradition of stage doormen who sit at tiny desks in tiny offices right next to the stage door. They monitor who comes in and out and keep track of deliveries. They keep out people who shouldn't be there and help people who should be there get where they're going. The stage doorman knows everything. He usually hears it all—intentional or not. Stage doormen can be the sweetest people in the world, and they always get a lot of respect from the cast.

Also at the stage door you'll find the call board, which is a backstage bulletin board that contains information about the production, including schedules for rehearsals and special notices. Everyone knows that it's their responsibility to check the call board every day. If it's posted there, you are responsible for knowing it. Theaters are too big to chase people down to tell them something. If there's news from the stage manager, actors find out at the call board.

Finally, at the stage door, actors initial the sign-in sheet. Professional actors are required to be in the theater thirty minutes before the show starts. Some come earlier, but the rule is they must be there by "half hour." At thirty minutes to curtain, the stage manager checks the sign-in sheet to make sure everyone is in the theater. If someone has not signed in, preparations need to be made to put an understudy on. Lateness is never tolerated in the theater. Too many people are depending on you. *Including the audience!*

Courtney Reed signs programs on a cold night.

Stephanie Levin, David Kaley

David Kaley

WARDROBE ROOM

The people who maintain and prepare the costumes for each performance work for the **wardrobe department**. These people work very hard to clean, maintain, and (if needed) repair the costumes before each performance and place them where they need to be. Some costumes are very elaborate and need daily attention. Buttons need to be sewn on, beads and sequins reattached, and zippers mended. All of this happens in and around the wardrobe room.

I have never been in a wardrobe room that didn't have a washing machine going. There is always laundry to do, and between costumes, undergarments, and the towels used to clean up after every show, the washing machine never gets any rest.

The wardrobe department is also responsible for getting the actors dressed. It is absolutely true that at home you are expected to get yourself dressed, and rightly so. But you don't have to get into a corset, or a flying harness, or a huge costume that lights up—that's what the wardrobe department is there to help with.

Very often, the wardrobe department doesn't deliver the costumes to the dressing rooms. Often they get preset around the stage for quick changes during the show. Frequently, actors race offstage and have to change their clothes in a matter of seconds. Shirts that open from the back with neckties attached to the front are torn off. An elaborate dress drops to the floor, and the actress steps right out of it and into another one. It gets lifted up and zipped with only seconds to spare before she races back onstage looking as if she were calmly entering on another day in the story. The wardrobe department conducts it all, and becomes very close to the actors.

Wardrobe people know when a sip of water is part of the costume change, or that on that particular night a cough drop is just the thing to keep the curtain up. Wardrobe people wear a sort of sewing version of a construction tool belt and are ready for anything from a torn costume to an actress who isn't feeling well and just needs to throw up before she goes back onstage. And yes, that happens—more often than you'd think!

WIG ROOM

The **hair department** manages the wig room. It is no surprise that the wig room is where all the hair—wigs, mustaches, beards, sideburns, and occasionally hairy dog puppets—gets maintained.

For a big show like *Aladdin* or *Frozen*, there are literally hundreds of wigs in the wig room. Everyone needs their own custom-made wig, and frequently wigs get changed several times during the course of the show if the actor plays many different parts. Also, for each part played onstage, there are three people ready to play it, so that no matter who gets sick or goes on vacation, the show always goes on. And all three get their own wigs! Lining the walls of the wig room are shelves full of wigs, all sitting on wig heads—which are like human-size doll heads with no faces.

Wigs can be very simple or very elaborate, and the hair department keeps them looking great. Every night at *Tarzan*®, for example, the female lead Jane's wig gets reset so that it looks just as fresh the next day. It's like a very fast-paced beauty parlor in there.

Wigs also get worn out, and new actors are always coming into the show, so just keeping track of what wig is on what person, which wigs are in the dryer, and which wigs need to be combed out is a big job. Now say "which wigs" ten times fast.

The hair department could easily get "wigged out" if they weren't organized.

James Brown III, Angie Jerbasi

Ashley Blanchett

Patti Murin

The Lord of the Flies

In big theaters, "flying" objects—lights, scenery, curtains, or props—are some of the most important tools of staging a play. Above the stage and out of sight of the audience is a **fly tower**, or **fly loft**. This is a huge open area often as big and tall as the stage itself. It's like a box on top of a box. If there's a twenty-foot-tall wall used as scenery on the stage, that scenery can "fly" twenty feet up inside the fly tower and not be seen by the audience until it is lowered back to the stage again. So the fly loft is kind of like an attic where you store things away while they're not being used.

There are two basic ways to make such magic—one is with machines, and one is by hand. To fly things out onto the stage by hand, ropes or cables are attached to the scenery, lighting, or even a person. Those ropes go through a pulley and eventually end up tied near the wall offstage. If you pull the rope, the object goes into the air. If you let go, it comes crashing down. That sounds like a disaster waiting to happen, doesn't it?

AHOY, MATEY! IT'S CURTAIN TIME!

Hundreds of years ago, stage designers wanted to have elaborate scene changes, but they didn't have any of the technology we do today to make them happen. Flying scenery in and out of view of the audience was a clever but complicated idea. That's why sailors were hired to develop ways to use flies safely, just like raising and lowering the sails of a boat. In fact, a number of things in the theater are based on ships. The ropes and cables we use are called rigging, just like on a sailboat. Did you know the stage floor is called a deck, just like the floor of a boat?

For this reason, it is also considered bad luck for an actor to whistle on or offstage. Sailors used to use whistles to communicate with each other on board ships. Hundreds of years ago, an actor whistling backstage might have mistakenly cued one of the sailors to drop a sandbag that could land right on someone's head!

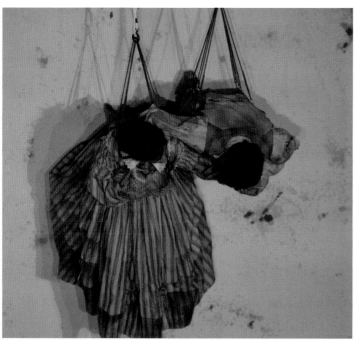

Well, it would be a disaster if the flies were not carefully engineered to balance the weight with what's called a counterweight system. The counterweight system makes sure that the weight of what is flying is carefully balanced at the other end of the rope. The flyman is the person in charge of pulling the ropes to make things go up and down, perfectly on cue—and gently, so they don't crash. This takes a lot of practice, and since safety always comes first in the theater, a great deal of care goes into preparing lines for flying.

The other system of flying uses machines called winches. These machines pull up and lower cable by winding and unwinding it, sort of like a giant fishing reel. The motor unspools, letting more cable out and lowering the object. It can then reverse and wind the cable back onto the spool and raise the object. These motors are run by computers.

Kara Madrid, Michael Hollick

For *Tarzan*®, these actors had to learn to walk down a wall with a rope holding them up. It's harder than it looks!

Stage Notes

* *Peter Pan* is one of the most beloved stories in modern theater, but few people know that it also started a revolution in stage flying. In 1950, a young Englishman named Peter Foy sailed from London to New York to stage the flying for a Broadway play of *Peter Pan*. The show was so thrilling that the story was reimagined as a musical just a few years later, and in 1954, Peter Foy famously returned to Broadway to fly Mary Martin as Peter Pan. Peter's company, Flying by Foy, became the standard of flying in the theater. Foy's flying systems have been used in *Beauty and the Beast, Aida, The Lion King, Tarzan®,* and *Mary Poppins*.

* Pichón Baldinu created the extraordinary flying moves in *Tarzan®*, but he became famous for the ingenious theater company he cofounded in Argentina called De La Guarda. With this renegade theater company, he created some of the most imaginative stage flying ever seen. It was his approach with bungee cords and rock-climbing gear that caused *Tarzan®* director Bob Crowley to ask him to create the flying and aerial gymnastics for *Tarzan®*.

* In the stage version of *Mary Poppins*, Bert the chimney sweep tap-dances upside down on the ceiling. The technique is the same as a flying rig, but the result is something that had never happened on Broadway before!

FLYING!

Many Disney shows have had to fly actors on Broadway. In London in the late 1600s, "Restoration Spectaculars" were very elaborate stage productions that often had scenes of flying actors who arrived in the shows like angels with magnificent wings stuck to their backs and huge ropes attached to them from above.

When Mary Poppins flies up in the air with her famous umbrella, or when Peter Pan flies across the stage, the audience is meant to believe that it is some sort of magic that is lifting them up—even when we of course can see the wires. After all, nobody can really fly. And if they can fly, they certainly aren't wasting their time working in the theater!

Another kind of flying, or aerial work (*aerial* means "in the air"), is used in *Tarzan®*. In that show, the actors are like rock climbers, and they attach themselves to ropes or stretchy bungee cords to lift or bounce themselves up the walls. There is no attempt made to hide the wires. You are supposed to see them, just as you see the famous vine that all Tarzans swing on in the movies.

No matter whether it is meant to be an illusion, or intended that you see how it is done, all flying is pretty much the same—and a lot of fun to do. The actor wears a very secure (and often heavy) harness under his costume. It has special metal connectors that the cables attach to. Flying people in shows can be dangerous and requires a great deal of caution and many safety procedures, but it is always fun for the audience—especially when the actors fly right over them!

Argentinian aerial designer Pichón Baldinu created all the flying effects for *Tarzan®*.

DID YOU KNOW?

Sometimes stage flying is meant to be an illusion. In *Aida*, there was a set design for a swimming pool as seen from above. The audience saw the pool as if they were in the sky looking down at it, and it looked like two girls were swimming across the pool. In actuality, cables raised and lowered them in the air.

Puppets

Almost everyone now knows about the extraordinary puppets in *The Lion King*. Those creations by Julie Taymor and Michael Curry have revolutionized Broadway theater.

But puppets have long been their own form of theater around the world, like Punch and Judy, or like Japan's Bunraku theater. Puppets have also often appeared in shows to simulate live animals or to serve as stand-ins for live actors.

Frozen uses two completely different types of puppets each night.

Olaf appears as a puppet with a visible actor. The human performer is fully visible to the audience, and they watch both her *and* the puppet, designed by Michael Curry. The design is based on the film but is also a theatrical interpretation of the character.

Max Casella

105

SVEN

Sven in *Frozen* is a particularly complicated puppet/costume. At one point during the process of making the Broadway version of *Frozen*, we very seriously considered cutting the character altogether, because we had no idea how it could be done or how he could fit into the show.

Thank goodness director Michael Grandage was excited to explore the idea with puppet designer Michael Curry, because Sven is one of the most beautiful creations in the show.

Rob Ashford,
Lorenzo Pisoni,
Andrew Pirozzi

The full-scale Sven figure was designed to be performed by a single actor. The role was created by Andrew Pirozzi, an actor who has been dancing since he was four and learned tumbling and hand balancing studying at circus school and performing with an acrobatic team. Here Andrew shows how he "becomes" Sven.

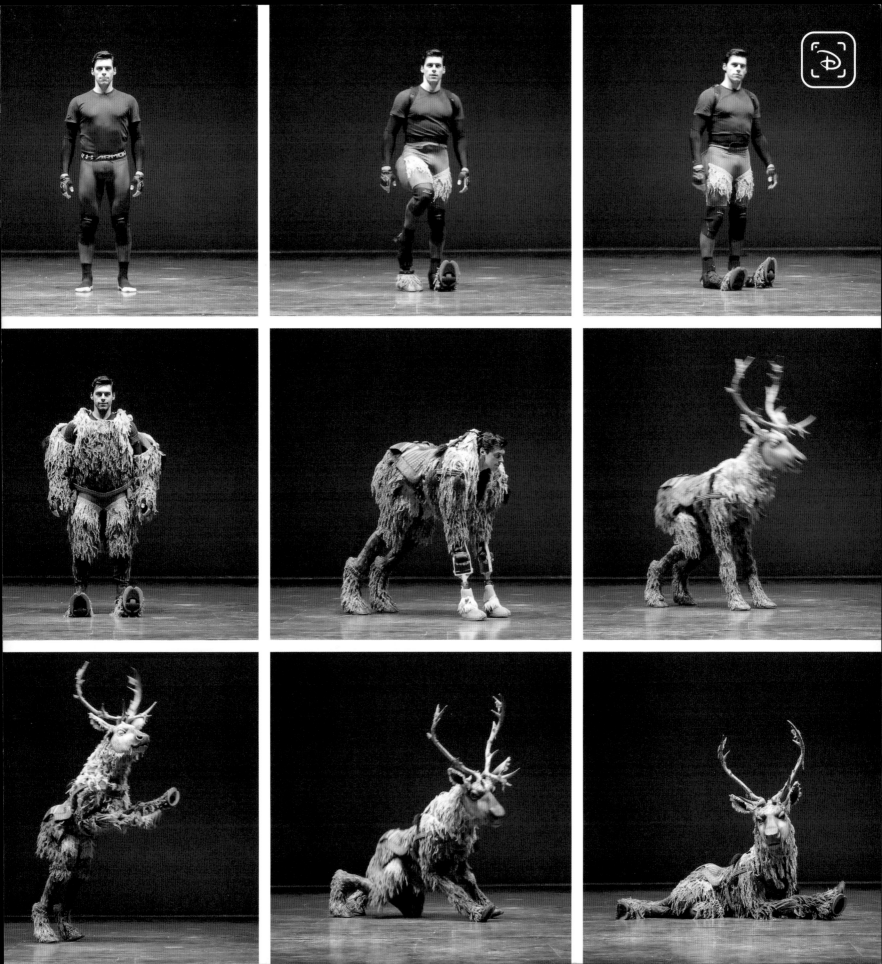

The Light Stuff

Sample swatches of gels (above) can turn light many different colors.

AIDA SAND DUNE

AIDA SILK LINES

AIDA PALMS

The gobos create patterns of light onstage.

DID YOU KNOW?

Frozen uses traditional lights, as well as LED lights, as well as projectors, as well as tiny little video monitors embedded behind translucent scenery to create the lighting for the show.

In ancient Greece, live theater was performed in daylight, so theaters were built in the open air and the lighting was taken care of by the sun. The ancient Romans came next, and they were probably the first to use torches and lamps for nighttime performances. Over two thousand years later, colored lights and fancy ways to move the lighting around became part of the theater.

Most early lighting required some sort of fire, like oil lamps, candles, and torches, to produce the special effects that audiences loved. They were also very dangerous, and back in those days theaters were constantly catching on fire. It's a good thing the electric lightbulb was invented, because now, lighting is a lot more fun and a lot less dangerous!

Caissie Levy

INSTRUMENTS, LAMPS, AND ELECTRICS: WHAT'S WHAT?

Everything we call lighting is part of the electrics department. The thing that projects the light itself is called a lighting **instrument**.

Inside the lighting instrument is the **lamp**. The lamp in the theater is what you call a lightbulb at home. What you call a lamp at home, we call an instrument in the theater. Got it? Good, because that part always confuses me. Read it again and see if you get it.

Frozen projection and video designer Finn Ross.

Natasha Katz has designed lights for *Beauty and the Beast, Aida, On the Record, Tarzan®, The Little Mermaid, Aladdin,* and *Frozen.* We like her a lot!

Of course, today we have both traditional incandescent bulbs in the theater as well as LED instruments. LED, which stands for light-emitting diode, is a new form of lighting.

You likely have LED lights at home, too, because they use much less electricity to light up a room, and it takes much less electricity to compensate for or "cool off" the heat that traditional lights produce. As we all try to be "greener," LEDs become a bigger part of life.

The next thing you need is something to control the color of the light. Most lights do this with some sort of color filter, or what's called a **gel**, that the light passes through. (Think of these as sort of like sunglasses for the lights.) As the beam of light shoots out, the light turns whatever color the filter is. There are many different types of color filters made of different materials.

LED lights, on the other hand, do not use gels or filters. The actual LED can change color based on what the computerized board (or at home, your smartphone) tells it to do. Many lighting designers don't yet like the color produced by LED instruments as much as traditional lighting. I don't think they are wrong, but LED will become the standard and get better and better, and we will become more accustomed to them. And the *earth* will thank us for using less energy when we make theatrical magic!

You can also control the "shape" of the light by using a **gobo**. A gobo is a thin circular plate with holes cut in it that goes into the lighting instrument to create patterns of projected light. Imagine if you took a piece of foil and cut a star shape out of it, then put it over the end of a flashlight. When you point the flashlight at the wall, you'll see a star. That's what a gobo does.

Finally, you need some way to control all the instruments so the lights come up or dim to a certain brightness at a certain speed. To do this, you use a **lighting board**. Dimmers are part of the lighting board. They are just like the switches in your house that allow you to make the light brighter or dimmer. The exact same concept is used in the theater, except no one is there yelling at you to "stop playing with those lights!"

Disney
FROZEN
THE BROADWAY MUSICAL

ST JAMES THEATRE
NEW YORK, NY

DIRECTED BY: MICHAEL GRANDAGE
CHOREOGRAPHED BY: ROB ASHFORD
SCENERY AND COSTUMES BY: CHRISTOPHER ORAM
LIGHTING BY: NATASHA KATZ
SOUND BY: PETER HYLENSKI
SPECIAL FX BY: JEREMY CHERNICK

Drawing Title:	
LIGHT PLOT	

Drawn By:	Scale [Except Where Noted]:
AP	1/2"=1'-0"
Filename:	Issue Date:
Frozen - NY Light Plot v2015	05/28/2018
Sheet No:	
LT-01	
	OF 9

WHAT ARE WE GOING TO LIGHT?

Houselights: **Houselights** brighten the auditorium so the audience doesn't trip over each other or the seats. Houselights can be very elaborate and beautiful, or they can be simple lights that can be turned on and off like in a school classroom.

    Traditional Lighting: There are two types of traditional lighting instruments: lights that **flood** or **wash** an area of the stage with light, and lights that illuminate very specific areas on the stage, or **spots**. These lights are positioned all around the theater, including "in the house" (facing the stage from the front), backstage (facing toward the stage), and even above the stage, pointing down.

    Moving Lights: It used to be that lights were positioned and locked down with clamps to point at just one area. Today, there are lights that have motors inside them that move all by themselves without anyone there to guide them. A computer sends a signal to the light and it moves to a preprogrammed location. When you see lots of beams of light sweeping the stage at the same time, you know you are seeing computerized **moving lights**.

    Follow Spots: There are lighting instruments that work like very bright, gigantic flashlights. An operator controls the light, aims it at a specific actor, and follows him wherever he goes. Follow spots are useful to make sure that an actor never steps into a dark area, and also to make clear to the audience who the star is by keeping him in the brightest light no matter where he goes.

    Today there is special technology that allows a follow spot to follow a performer even when no one is there to move the light. The actor wears a transmitter that "talks" to the follow spot so it knows where she is. As she moves, it moves. This technology is in an early stage, but will probably become a standard way of using certain follow spots in the future. Being a great follow spot operator is a skilled craft all its own, but this automation will likely make it easier to follow actors making simple moves.

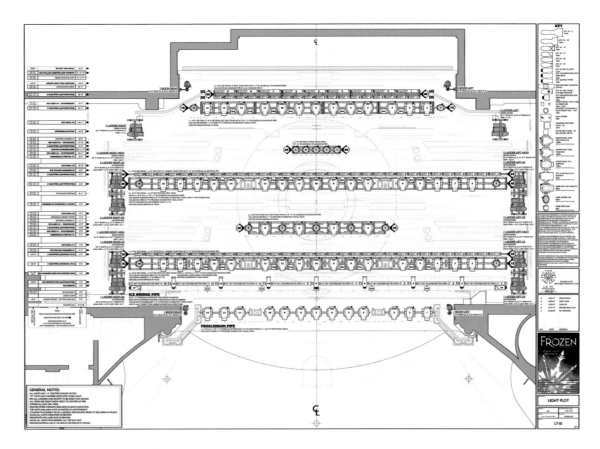

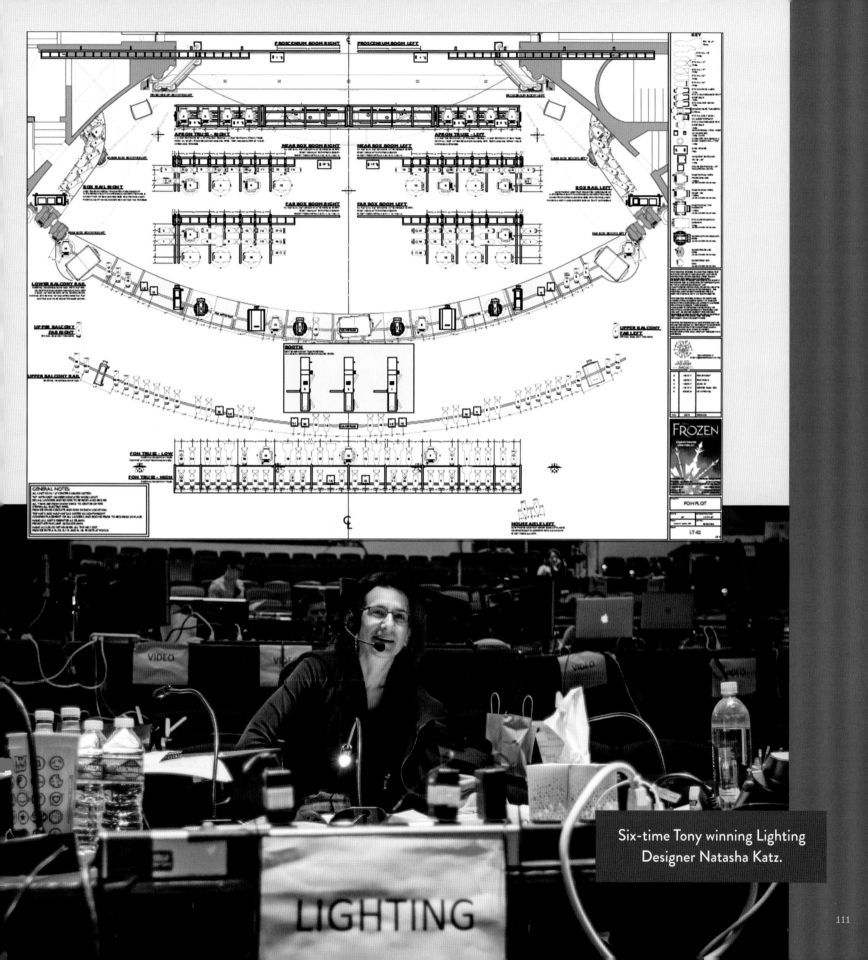

Six-time Tony winning Lighting Designer Natasha Katz.

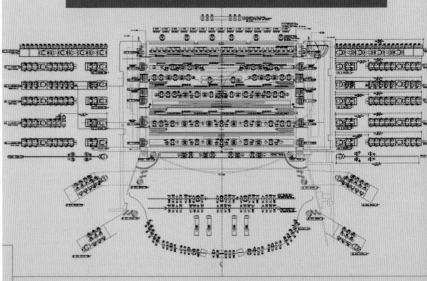

Sierra Bogges

See how different these three scenes from *The Little Mermaid* look, all because of lighting?

Sherie Rene Scott

This diagram (below) of a light plot from *The Little Mermaid* shows where each light is placed.

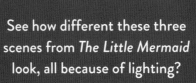

Ghost Light: The **ghost light** is a single lightbulb that stands glowing on the stage in every empty theater. The last thing you do in the theater before locking up at night is put the ghost light downstage center and turn it on.

Despite its mysterious name, this light is a safety device to make sure that a theater, with all its dangers, is never left in the dark. If there weren't a ghost light, the first guy who arrived in the morning would stand a good chance of falling through a trapdoor or stumbling into the open orchestra pit. Then *he* just might become a ghost!

Caissie Levy

LIMELIGHT

No one uses limelight anymore, but the expression "to be in the limelight" still refers to when someone is in the public eye. The expression comes from when actors used to be very visible onstage while standing in the limelight.

Lime is a powder that, when heated by a flame, glows brightly without ever catching on fire. If you put a reflector behind it, the glowing lime casts light onto the stage. Lime was popular before the invention of electric lighting and was yet another reason theaters were always burning down. The lime may not have caught fire when heated—but everything around it did!

You might be wondering why keeping fire out of the theater was such a hard idea to grasp in the old days. The answer is simple. Fire was used to create beauty onstage, and no one who has ever made theater is willing to compromise what they think will make the show great. Even if it means burning the place down!

When you think about lighting, you think about lighting the stage and what's on it, like people, scenery, props, or even the floor. But have you ever thought about lighting the air? Lighting designers frequently use a sort of fog or smoke effect onstage. When they shine beams of light through smoke, they can create patterns or color in the air. Best not to try this at home!

The ghost light (below) protects the theater and everyone in it.

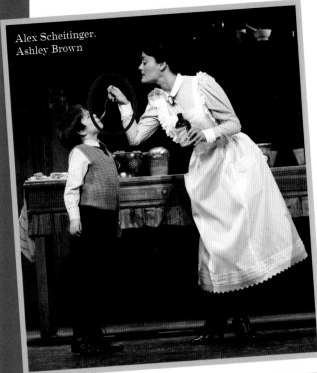

Alex Scheitinger,
Ashley Brown

Props

A **prop** is any object held, manipulated, or carried by a performer during a theatrical performance. It is short for "property." If someone grabbed your bag and took your stuff, you might say, "Hey! Leave that alone! It is my property." Well, in the theater everything that isn't scenery or costumes is a property, or prop. A vase of flowers is a prop. A cane is a prop. A bottle of cola is a prop. It doesn't need to be the real thing, and in fact, the real thing often doesn't work as well as a fake. What's important is how it looks, or "reads," from out front. Props can even look silly close-up, but what matters is how they look to the audience.

There are lots of tricks to props. They often are specially designed to create an effect—like a bag of groceries that breaks open at the bottom just as an actress walks in the door. In *Aladdin*, big magic tricks, like the trunk that makes Aladdin disappear, or small tricks that allow actors to snap their fingers and produce little bursts of fire, are all props.

Prop food is always interesting. Eating onstage is difficult to do because you need to keep talking, and on top of that, many actors are very fussy about what they eat and when. As much as possible, actors try to pretend they are eating when they can get away with it. If they do have to eat, the prop department sorts exactly what it will be and how it will look and taste. It is best not to get your hopes up about how it will taste.

Props also need to be carefully organized backstage. Nothing is worse than not being able to find your prop before you run onstage. There are legendary stories in the theater about props that don't work or go missing during the show. Nothing is worse at the time it happens, and nothing is funnier a few years later.

Sierra Bogges,
J.J. Singleton

Every Disney show has a few iconic props, like Mary Poppins' Bottle and Spoon, Ariel's dinglehopper, and Anna and Elsa's Toy Olaf!

Ayla Schwartz,
Audrey Bennett

PROPERTY MASTER

The property master creates, finds, organizes, and manages the props for the show. It is a very complicated job and on some shows requires the work of several people in the prop department, from designers to people who run the show. Sometimes they have crazy jobs that you would not expect. Some shows are very prop-oriented.

Aladdin's lamp, an enchanted rose, and this magical, breakable hourglass from *Freaky Friday* are all called props onstage.

Emma Hunton, Heidi Blickenstaff

Stage Notes

✳ *Aladdin* has 268 props onstage, from a magic lamp that produces smoke, to swords for fights (as well as "swallowing"), to magic tricks for the Genie and his crew, to Aladdin's (rubber) loaf of bread that he shares with the beggar woman every night.

✳ Although Elsa's beautiful costumes in *Frozen* are maintained and managed each night by the wardrobe crew, it is actually a member of the props crew who partners with the actress to create the amazing illusion in "Let It Go" where she changes her dress in one second.

✳ The elephant that walks down the aisle nightly in *The Lion King* on Broadway is a prop that takes four actors inside it to make the journey. After it gets to the stage and makes its exit, it is stored for the rest of the show fifteen feet up in the air over the stage. It is too big to fit anywhere else.

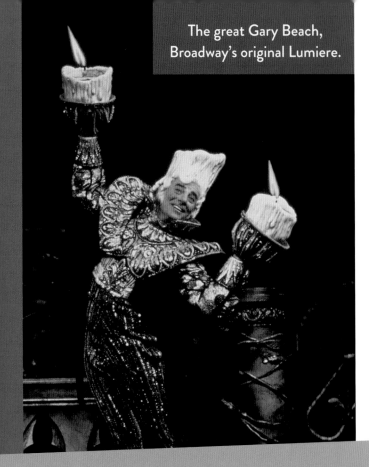

The great Gary Beach, Broadway's original Lumiere.

Special Effects

Special effects aren't the sole responsibility of any single department. Some special effects are part of the prop department. Others are part of lighting. Some are part of the costumes. **Special effects** are visual elements such as fog, smoke, lightning, breaking furniture, snow, or the like, that require special tricks to effect reality or fantasy on the stage.

Mattea Conforti, Ayla Schwartz

PYROTECHNICS

The illusion of fire and explosions is known in the theater as **pyrotechnics**, or "pyro" for short. Many shows have pyro effects. *Aladdin* has fireworks onstage at the end of the song "Friend Like Me" with real flying sparks, sort of like something you would see on the Fourth of July.

For as long as the theater has been around, flashes of fire and smoke have been used onstage to create a dynamic effect and to thrill audiences.

Special effects expert Jeremy Chernick.

There are live fireworks in *Aladdin* every night!

Josh Strickland.
Chester Gregory III

Actors have to be careful when their props involve fire!

117

MAGIC AND ILLUSION

Sometimes you need to perform magic tricks onstage. In the case of some Disney shows, this is required to give the impression that something impossible has been achieved, almost as if the performer had magic or supernatural powers. In *Aladdin* on Broadway, his magic carpet flies with a very complicated illusion technique. It took more than a year to figure out if it would be possible—and it thrills audiences nightly. We are all very proud of what Jim Steinmeyer, the illusion designer, created. I'm sure you'd love to know how those kinds of stage illusions are created, but a good magician never gives away his tricks! You'll just have to work in the theater to find out how it's done!

Magicians train a lifetime to perform tricks, but actors onstage need to learn them quickly, and directors need to figure out how to make those tricks happen. That's when you call in a specialist to create the illusions for the show.

Ashley Brown

Mary Poppins uses stage magic to pull many things out of her carpetbag, including a four-foot-tall potted palm!

Henry Hodges, Ashley Brown

Being a good technical director requires a lot of experience and a very cool head. Nobody is better than Geoff Quart.

Putting It All Together

TECHNICAL DIRECTOR

The **technical director** is responsible for the delivery and operation of all technical aspects of the production. It is a challenging and exciting job. Of course, like many aspects of the theater, if everything goes brilliantly, very few people notice what a good job the tech director did. If the scenery crumbles to the floor, everyone blames the tech director.

Technical directors have to know about all aspects of backstage life, from carpentry, to electrics, to props, to automated scenery, to you name it. If it is onstage and it doesn't have a heartbeat, it is the responsibility of the technical director. Technical directors come to the job from many different areas of the theater, but the great ones, like Geoff Quart, take on the job because they love to see things run well. The satisfaction of solving problems and making things run smoothly fuels the best people in the business.

STAGE MANAGEMENT TEAM

Stage managers are the lifeblood of rehearsing, running, and maintaining a show. They are in charge of the rehearsal room and call each rehearsal to order. They work with the director to plan the rehearsal process and are responsible for making the rehearsal room look, feel, and operate as though the actual show were taking place.

Stage managers maintain the script and integrate all new scenes and songs into it. They also balance between the technical and artistic worlds. The stage manager learns the show intimately and, with the director, creates the "flow" of the production. It is one of the stage managers who, during each rehearsal, follows the prompt script and "calls the cues" for the lights and scene changes. Everyone in the theater waits for the stage manager to say "Go!" before they execute the next lighting cue or scenic change. In a song called "Friend Like Me" from *Aladdin*, cues come fast and furious, and the stage manager is in constant verbal contact with the crew onstage and out front to make it all happen. She wears a headset so she can hear everything the crew needs to tell her, and she has a microphone to talk to each of them. During the song, the lights are changing, follow spots are following, gold towers are turning, and fireworks are exploding—all under the control of the stage manager, who calls cues every second of the song. On a big show, the stage manager has a series of TV monitors showing all different angles of the stage and the wings to make sure everyone and everything is in place before she says "Go!"

Every show is different, and each stage manager and stage management team divides up the job differently, but from the time everyone walks through the stage door to the final curtain, the stage manager is in charge of the production. It is her job to keep the pace of the cues, to protect the actors and the crew, to be mindful of problems that might be ahead, and to solve problems as they come up.

If you want to know what's going on in a theater, ask the stage manager. Many directors and producers began their careers as stage managers. It is one of the few areas that touch almost every aspect of the production, from script and design, to actors, wardrobe, makeup, wigs, and lighting. Stage managers are generally not responsible for anything "out in the house," meaning anything dealing with the public except coordinating with the house manager about starting the show.

OLAF
Oh no. The fire's out!

Olaf Toss Match   **91**

LTS 436 (Fire Finger, Fireplace)
ADECK 555 – Red
Portal 2 SR OFF

ANNA
Careful, Olaf!

OLAF
Whoa. So that's heat. I love it! So, where's Hans? What happen--Ooh! But don't touch it! So, where's Hans? What happened to your kiss?

ANNA
I was wrong about him. It wasn't true love. Please Olaf, you can't stay here. You'll melt.

OLAF
I am not leaving here until we find some other act of true love to save you… Got any ideas?

ANNA
I don't even know what love is.

OLAF
That's okay, I do… Love is putting someone else's needs before yours, you know, like, how Kristoff brought you back here to Hans and left you forever.

ANNA
Kristoff loves me?

OLAF
Wow, you really don't know anything about love, do you?

ANNA
Olaf, you're melting.

OLAF
Some people are **WORTH** melting for.

Just maybe not right this second. It's okay. I've got it.

(MORE)

WARN
AutoDECK
560 – Red
Arendelle Window SR OPEN
565 – Blue
Arendelle Window SR CLOSE
AF 568: Shutters CLOSE
570 – Yellow
Arendelle Portal 1 OFF
575 – Green
Settee OFF SL Track 1
Fireplace OFF SL Track 2
AutoFLY
910 – Red
Ice Walls 1, 2, 3 IN to Mid
Arendelle Portal 2 OUT
Overhead LX 4 & 5 OUT to Default
Overhead LX 7 IN to Default
LL #2 SL/SR DS IN to Low
Safety Check / Conditionals Only
920 – Blue
Safety Check / Conditionals Only
IN 1 LIGHT
FLATTEN Fireplace

ADECK 560 – Red
SR Window OPEN

Window Opening

LTS 437 (Fog Wall ON, US Fog)

Take a look at this page from the prompt script to see how many "cues" Stage Manager Lisa Dawn Cave calls during this scene in *Frozen*.

WHAT'S MY CUE?

A cue is a prompt that the stage manager gives to someone so that they do something at the right moment. There are several types of cues. Light cues are the various changes the board operator makes to the lights. If there are 248 light cues in the show, the lighting changes that many times. There can be a cue for a piece of scenery to move to a different place between scene changes. There are also cues for actors. The director might say, "Your cue to enter is when you hear the gun go off." If the gun doesn't actually go off, things get a little out of whack, so cues are important because they keep things moving smoothly. When there's no other way to communicate with the person who's supposed to do something, the stage manager will use "cue lights," which are little lights that go on to signal a cue.

STAGE CREW

There are three key stage crew departments that run what happens on the stage (in addition to wardrobe, which we discussed earlier). Each of these departments has a "head," known on Broadway as house heads. If you have great house heads, you are a lucky producer.

The stage crew departments are:

Electrics: This team manages everything that has electricity running to it. They are responsible, of course, for running the lighting and maintaining the lighting instruments, the lighting board, and also all the sound equipment. The lighting board operator, the soundboard operator, the follow spot operators, and all electricians on the deck are part of the electrics department. When the stage gets smoky to create a cool lighting effect, it's the electrics department running the machine that makes the smoke and light. If it lights up, turns on, or has a switch, it is probably part of electrics.

HERE'S AN EXERCISE:

During a scene change, an elevator comes up from the basement, and on it there is a "room" created onstage by the following items:

1. A door frame with a swinging door in it

2. A table with a tray, teacups, and a pot of tea

3. A flickering candle

4. A floor lamp that the actor will turn on

5. A chair with a sweater on it that the leading man will put on during the scene

6. A pile of dirty laundry

Can you figure out which department is responsible for putting each thing in place and taking care of it?

HERE ARE THE ANSWERS....

1. The door frame belongs to carpentry.

2. The table, teacups, pot of tea, and the tea itself are props.

3. The flickering candle belongs to props if it is a real flame and to electrics if it is a fake candle with a "flicker" bulb.

4. The floor lamp is the responsibility of props, but the electrics department is in charge of making sure that it's plugged in and working.

5. The chair is the responsibility of props, but the sweater is the responsibility of the wardrobe department.

6. The pile of dirty laundry is a prop as long as no one wears it. If someone has to put it on, wardrobe is in charge.

Props: The prop department manages the props and also sets the props up, whether they are preset in the wings or put onstage before the curtain goes up. The prop department works with the set designer to create the props and maintain them for the run of the show. If you pick it up, eat it, hit someone with it, shoot it, swing it, carry it, or toss it, the prop department is responsible for it. They are also responsible for maintaining a clean stage floor and for miscellaneous furniture backstage, like chairs and tables. People in the prop department are exceptionally handy. Everyone would like a good prop person at home to help around the house.

Mike Allen is the head carpenter on *Frozen*. How can you be a carpenter on a set that's made of high-tech resin?

Victor Amerling, head of the prop department, sweeps up the flower petals he showers onto the *Mary Poppins* set every night.

Carpentry: At home, carpenters build stuff out of wood, but in the theater the carpentry department includes the people who manage the big stuff. They are in charge of the scenery and the machines that make the scenery move around the stage. If it flies onto the stage, carpentry is responsible for what is flying (even if it is a person), as well as the thing that makes it fly. The carpentry department is responsible for elevators and, of course, the scenery on the elevators. Trapdoors and the entire deck itself belong to the carpentry department. If you can fall into it, fall from it, or fall through it, the carpentry department is probably responsible for it.

Stage Notes

STAGE SUPERSTITIONS

Superstitions have always played a large role in the theater. Maybe it's because it is so hard to tell why shows are successful; maybe it's because it's so scary to go out there and perform; or maybe it's because theaters are like old houses with lots of history, ghosts, and spirits in them. Superstitions can be anything from not wanting to say the last line of a play before the first audience comes, to not wanting to rehearse the curtain call before the final rehearsal, to wearing a pair of "lucky socks" on opening night. No matter what an actor's superstition may be, NEVER tell a superstitious actor he's crazy. He already knows that. He became an actor!

Here are a couple of famous stage superstitions:

❋ **Mac-Shuuush!**

Shakespeare's famous tragedy *Macbeth* is said to be cursed, and to avoid problems, actors never say the title of the play out loud when inside a theater or a theatrical space (like a rehearsal room or costume or scene shop). Since the play is set in Scotland, the secret code you say when you need to say the title of the play is "the Scottish play." If you do say the title by accident, legend has it you have to go outside, turn around three times, and come back into the theater. Just don't say it, and you'll be fine.

❋ **Breaking a Leg Is Good?**

In the theater it is considered bad luck to wish people good luck. So if you want to wish someone good luck in the theater, you have to wish them bad luck instead by saying, "Break a leg." The idea is that no matter what you say, the fates will turn against it, so if you wish bad luck, it'll turn to good! Frankly, most people don't know why they say it, but everyone says "Break a leg" before a show, and no one says "Good luck." Ever. If you think that's crazy, many French performers whisper a dirty word for "poop" in your ear and then kiss you on the cheek before you go onstage.

Lucky socks?

Rehearsal for *The Hunchback of Notre Dame*, Jesuit High School.

ENCORE Stuff That Will Be Useful
After You Finish Reading This Book

Putting On a Play

There are many ways to put on a play at school or at home. You can set your garage or your classroom up, write a play of your own, and invite your friends or other students to get involved. All you need is a story to tell.

There are also many plays that have already been written, and those are fun to produce and act in as well. Two of the best places to go to learn about the shows you can *license* to produce yourself are **Music Theatre International** and **Samuel French**. They have catalogs (printed and online) that you can explore. When I was starting in the theater, I would spend hours reading the catalogs of the plays that I wanted to put on. Now, many of our Disney musicals are at Music Theatre International, and you can put on your own versions of *Aladdin, The Jungle Book, The Lion King, Newsies, Beauty and the Beast, Mary Poppins*, and even *Frozen*.

(top) *Beauty & the Beast JR*, Medford Memorial Middle School. (bottom) *High School Musical*, Flagship Summer Theatre

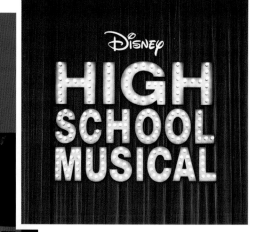

WHAT IS LICENSING?

Licensing is the process of acquiring the "rights" to a show. Think of it as permission to act and sing the songs that artists have spent years crafting into a stage show.

Picking a Show and Getting the Script

Picking a show is the start of all the fun. It's figuring out what characters and songs you want to bring to life onstage. Maybe you'll enjoy organizing Belle's greetings to the townspeople in *Beauty and the Beast*, or figuring out how to make the magic carpet fly in *Aladdin JR.*, Or think of how much fun all that snow from *Frozen JR.* will be during your summer production.

You can license different versions of famous musicals. You want to pick what's right for your production.

First, there are full-length musicals where you get to use the same scripts that actors and designers used on Broadway. Shows like Disney's *Beauty and the Beast*, *The Little Mermaid*, *Newsies*, *Tarzan*®, and *High School Musical* are all available to do in schools, community theater groups, and camps. Most of the shows come with Production Handbooks with useful tips on directing and designing your production and an option to purchase pre-recorded music tracks for performance.

If you are just starting to put on shows, Broadway Junior® musicals are a great way to start. These shows include a ShowKit® of materials, including a Director's Guide with tips on staging and setting up a rehearsal schedule, rehearsal and performance tracks with full orchestras backing you up as you perform, choreography videos showcasing ideas on how to stage some of the production numbers, and other resources like sample budgets, press releases for marketing, and poster designs!

You can put on a show in most any space! Be creative—maybe use a gym and do a show in the round (perfect for creating an under-the-sea atmosphere for *The Little Mermaid*) or a production outside in a park (a perfect setting for *Tarzan*®). See page 20 for different ways to set up **your** theater!

For a step-by-step guide to putting on a show, you can visit:
www.disneytheatricallicensing.com

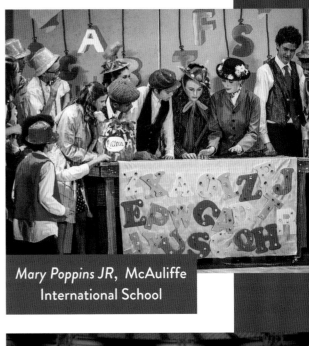

Mary Poppins JR, McAuliffe International School

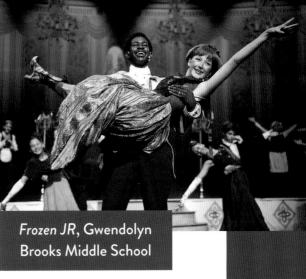

Frozen JR, Gwendolyn Brooks Middle School

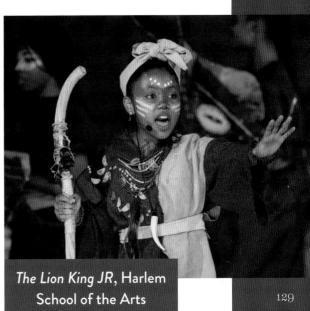

The Lion King JR, Harlem School of the Arts

129

Make a List; Check It Twice!

Here's a handy show checklist you can use to get your own production in the works!

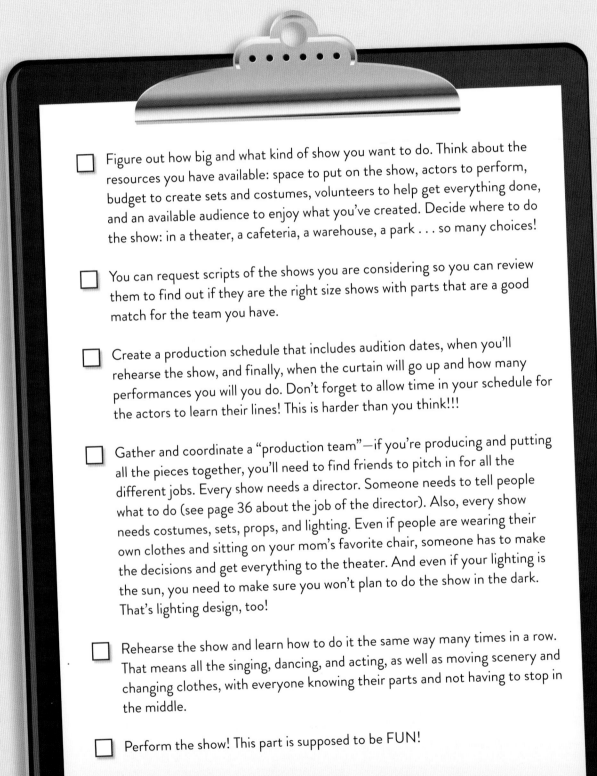

- ☐ Figure out how big and what kind of show you want to do. Think about the resources you have available: space to put on the show, actors to perform, budget to create sets and costumes, volunteers to help get everything done, and an available audience to enjoy what you've created. Decide where to do the show: in a theater, a cafeteria, a warehouse, a park . . . so many choices!

- ☐ You can request scripts of the shows you are considering so you can review them to find out if they are the right size shows with parts that are a good match for the team you have.

- ☐ Create a production schedule that includes audition dates, when you'll rehearse the show, and finally, when the curtain will go up and how many performances you will you do. Don't forget to allow time in your schedule for the actors to learn their lines! This is harder than you think!!!

- ☐ Gather and coordinate a "production team"—if you're producing and putting all the pieces together, you'll need to find friends to pitch in for all the different jobs. Every show needs a director. Someone needs to tell people what to do (see page 36 about the job of the director). Also, every show needs costumes, sets, props, and lighting. Even if people are wearing their own clothes and sitting on your mom's favorite chair, someone has to make the decisions and get everything to the theater. And even if your lighting is the sun, you need to make sure you won't plan to do the show in the dark. That's lighting design, too!

- ☐ Rehearse the show and learn how to do it the same way many times in a row. That means all the singing, dancing, and acting, as well as moving scenery and changing clothes, with everyone knowing their parts and not having to stop in the middle.

- ☐ Perform the show! This part is supposed to be FUN!

The Stage Isn't Just for Actors

This entire book is all about different people who work to put on a show. The stage isn't just about actors and acting. There are so many jobs that require so many different skills. The shiest person in the world can have a life of joy in the theater.

These are some of the jobs I've done in the theater starting back when I was in school and going all the way to getting to produce my first show on Broadway.

Director/Choreographer: *The Lion King KIDS*, Hull Jackson Montessori

Costume Designer: *The Hunchback of Notre Dame*, Jesuit High School

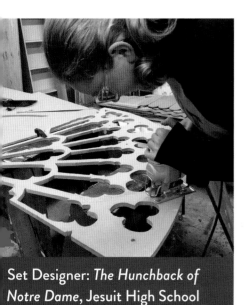

Set Designer: *The Hunchback of Notre Dame*, Jesuit High School

Lighting Crew: *Freaky Friday*, Bradford High School

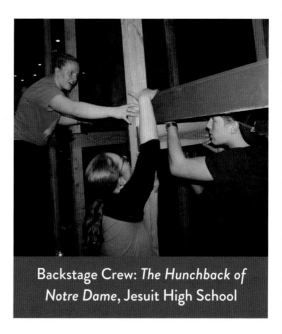

Backstage Crew: *The Hunchback of Notre Dame*, Jesuit High School

Don't Forget Your Theater-Speak!

BOOK: The script of a musical show.

CAST: The group of performers that appear in a show. To "cast" a show is to pick the actors.

CLOSING NOTICE: A dreadful sign that goes up to tell everyone that a play is closing in two weeks—which is the official amount of notice you must give professional actors. If you close with only one night's notice, you still have to pay the performers for two weeks. Most actors who do school and community plays rarely do the play longer than two weeks, so it really doesn't mean much to them!

CURTAIN CALL: The end of a show, when the cast bows in front of an audience that is clapping really loudly and screaming "Bravo!" Well, they don't always scream, but you do hope they clap.

"FIVE MINUTES": An announcement the stage manager makes to tell actors they have five minutes before getting to the stage for the first scene. Backstage, you'll hear, "Five minutes, ladies and gentlemen. Five minutes to places. This is your five-minute call." Sometimes just hearing those words really makes your heart race.

HIT: A very successful show. The opposite of a hit show is a flop. Nobody wants to produce or be in a flop, but it happens. Just ask me!

HOUSE SEATS: The "best" seats held back by a show so that friends of the producer, director, designers, and actors get good seats whenever they call. You have to know someone to get house seats. In reality, I prefer the seats in the front row of the mezzanine or balcony, and those are rarely house seats. Anyone can buy them!

INTERMISSION: This is the break between acts when the audience can get up and get a drink or go to the bathroom. Some shows don't have an intermission. Some shows have two of them.

LINE: Generally, in the theater, "lines" are the words actors say onstage. Actors often ask, "What's my first line in this scene?" or "When do I say that line?" Some actors count their lines to see if they have a good part. Smart actors are happy to have a part that is interesting whether they say a lot or not. Also, in rehearsals, actors will shout "Line!" when they forget what comes next, and then the stage manager says the line. The best actors never stop being "in character" when they call out for a line. They just hold the energy of the scene and continue once they get back on track.

MELODY: The part of a song that's just the music. For example, sing "Twinkle, Twinkle, Little Star." That's a song. Now hum it without the words. That is the melody of the song.

OPEN-ENDED RUN: A show that will keep performing until people stop coming. The opposite of an open-ended run is a limited engagement. That's when there are a fixed number of performances planned from the very beginning.

"PLACES": The stage manager says "Places!" to tell actors when to go to the stage and prepare for the curtain to go up. Everyone literally gets into the *place* they are supposed to be when it starts.

RUNNING TIME: How long the play takes to perform, including intermission. You might ask the house manager or box-office person what the running time is so you can arrange for a ride home after the show.

SET: The objects onstage when the actors are performing. A set can be elaborate and realistic, like a fancy house, or it can be a bunch of blue silk to make you think the play is happening in the sky, or it might be just a chair and a table. But whatever is on the stage is the set.

SOLD OUT: That's when all the tickets are gone and there are no more to sell.

STANDING OVATION: When the audience is so excited at the end of the show about what they saw that clapping just isn't enough, they often stand and clap. Everyone likes to get a standing ovation. I've done a couple of shows that got standing ovations *during* the show. In *Aladdin* on Broadway, the audience stood up to cheer the Genie and the cast at the end of "Friend Like Me." People talked about that!

STANDING ROOM ONLY: When there are no more seats, but the theater sells spaces at the back where you can stand and watch the show.

THE WINGS: The areas the audience can't see at stage right and stage left, where actors and crew get ready to go on or take things onstage.

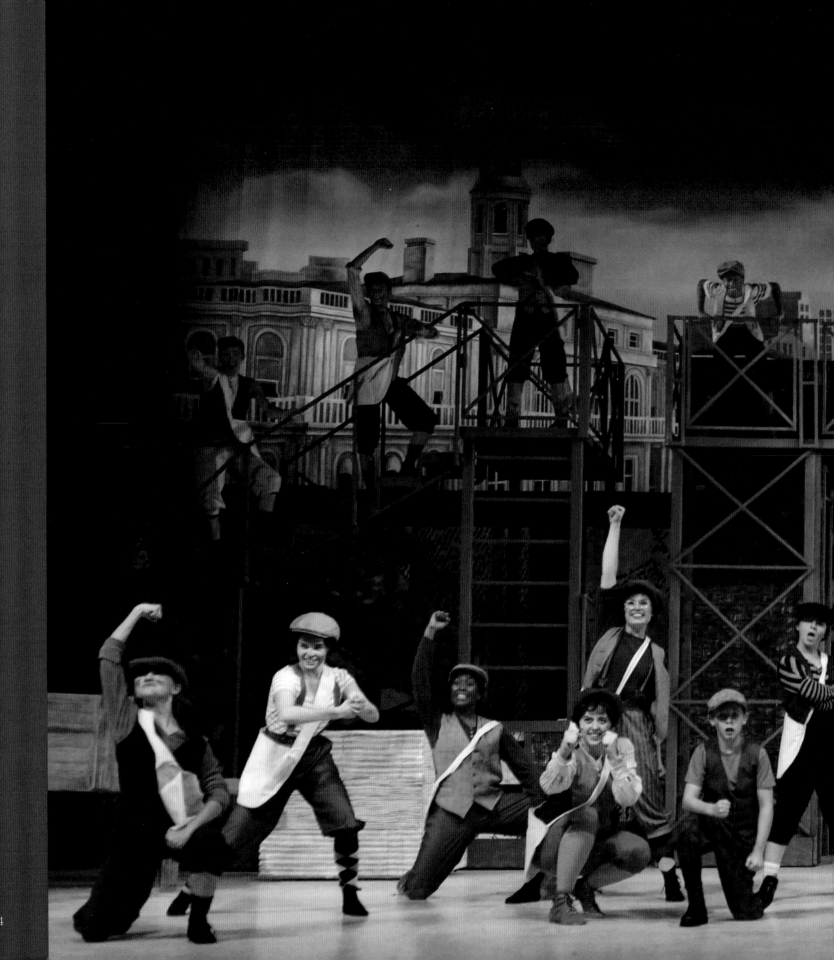

Afterword

When I wrote the first edition of *How Does the Show Go On?* back in 2007, I had no idea I'd hear from so many people who love the theater. I traveled across America speaking to fans and new friends and folks I never thought I'd meet. I talked to veteran theater artists who wanted to buy a copy for a young person, and to young people just discovering what the theater could mean to them. I heard from teachers, parents, students, and even people who thought they had no interest in theater.

I love working in the theater. And even though I feel sad if critics don't like what we've done, and lonely when I go far away from friends and family to work on something new, I've never felt more at home than I do in a theater working on a show.

In the theater, you are always learning. I learn when I see a show I love. I learn when I see a show that's not for me. I learn when colleagues bring new ideas to solve old problems. And I learn each time an audience sees a new show for the first time. I asked many of my theater friends to check over sections of this book, and they'd often say, "Hey, I didn't know that." It seems all of us have a lot to learn about our chosen craft. I know I still do.

Teachers have immeasurably enriched my life, and there is no one I'm more grateful for every time I enter a theater than the wonderful people who were and are my teachers, whether in school, in life, or in theater. My teachers were always there, and I feel lucky I got to know them.

If you have great teachers, listen to them. If you have a chance to be a teacher to someone, be one. And in the theater, never forget that you will *always* be a student.

101 Dalmatians KIDS, Children's Musical Theaterworks

Freaky Friday, Bradford High School

Photo Credits

Frozen rehearsal photos photographed at NEW 42nd STREET® Studios

Front cover: Deen Van Meer
Back cover: (Ashley Brown in *Mary Poppins*) Joan Marcus; (Michael James Scott in *Aladdin*, Caissie Levy and Patti Murin in *Frozen*, Jess LeProtto in *Newsies*, Jelani Alladin in *Frozen*) Deen Van Meer
Endpapers: (pictured from left to right) (Natasha Katz) Thomas Schumacher; (usher, patron) Disney Theatrical Group, (David Kaley) Marc Brenner; (James Monroe Iglehart in *Aladdin*) Deen Van Meer; (Caissie Levy, David Brian Brown in *Frozen*) Disney Theatrical Group; (Heather Headley in *Aida*) Joan Marcus; (Finn Ross) Disney Theatrical Group; (Courtney Reed, Gary Martori in *Aladdin*) Deen Van Meer; (Bob Crowley) Michael Le Poer Trench; (Stephen Oremus) Marc Brenner; (Ayla Schwartz, Audrey Bennett in *Frozen*) Deen Van Meer
Pages 2–3: Deen Van Meer
Page 5: Michael Carroll
Page 6: Private Collection by Thomas Schumacher
Page 7: Illustration by Scott Tilley
Pages 10–11: Disney Theatrical Group
Page 12: (top and bottom): Marc Brenner
Page 13: (top and bottom): Marc Brenner
Page 13: (right) © iStockphoto.com/byphoto
Page 14: (top): © iStockphoto.com/Murdo
Page 14: (right): Marc Brenner
Page 14: (bottom): Matthew Crockett
Page 15: (top): Phillip Jarrell
Page 15: (bottom): Disney Theatrical Group
Page 16: (top) Courtesy of Center Theatre Group/Mark Taper Forum
Page 16: (left) Mollie Boice
Page 16: (bottom) Daniellex Santana
Page 17: The Muny
Page 18: Hale Centre Theatre
Page 19: (bottom) Jane Hoffer/Courtesy of Lincoln Center Institute for the Arts in Education
Page 19: (top) Paul Silla/Porthouse Theatre, Kent State University
Page 21: (four images): Scott Tilley
Pages 22–23: Jenny Anderson
Page 24: (left) Disney Theatrical Group
Page 24: (right) Disney Theatrical Group
Pages 25–29: (all) Disney Theatrical Group
Page 30: Gino Domenico
Page 31: Disney Theatrical Group
Page 32: (top) Joan Marcus
Page 32: (bottom) Whitney Cox Photography Page 33: (Playbills): From PLAYBILL. Copyright © 1994, 1997, 2006, 2012, 2014, and 2018. Reprinted by permission of Playbill, Inc.
Page 34: (top) Disney Theatrical Group
Page 34: (bottom) Deen Van Meer
Page 35: (top) Deen Van Meer
Page 35: (center) Avi Gerver
Page 35: (bottom) Joan Marcus
Page 36: (top): Marc Brenner
Page 36: (bottom): Frank Veronsky
Page 37: (top) Provided by Rob Roth
Page 37: (center): Disney Theatrical Group
Page 37: (below center) Tammy Shell
Page 37: (bottom) Matthew Murphy
Page 38: (top) Lisa Crosby
Page 38: (bottom) 2006 Bruce Glikas
Page 39: (top) Tony Russell
Page 39: (bottom) Disney Theatrical Group
Page 39: (background) © iStockphoto.com/nickfree
Page 40: (top) Gerard Barnier
Page 40: (bottom left) Walt Disney Archives Photo Library
Page 40: (bottom right) © iStockphoto.com/cveltri
Page 41: (top left and bottom right) Disney Theatrical Group
Page 41: (top right) Marc Brenner
Page 41: (bottom left) Deen Van Meer
Page 42: (top left) Anita & Steve Shevett © 1998
Page 42: (top right) 2006 Bruce Glikas
Page 42: (bottom left) Disney Theatrical Group

Page 42: (bottom right) Johann Persson
Page 43: Johann Persson
Page 44: Disney Theatrical Group
Page 45: (top) Marc Brenner
Page 45: (bottom) Photo by Robert Townson
Page 46: (top and bottom) Marc Brenner
Page 47: (top) Kenneth Van Sickle
Page 47: (bottom left) © Getty Images
Page 47: (bottom left) Heidi Gutman
Page 48: Deen Van Meer
Page 49: (top) Johann Persson
Page 49: (bottom) Charles Erikson
Page 50: (top) Disney Theatrical Group
Page 50: (bottom) Walter McBride
Page 51: James Monroe Iglehart
Page 52: (top) Marc Brenner
Page 52: (bottom) Deen Van Meer
Page 53: (top and right) Christopher Oram
Page 53: (bottom) Disney Theatrical Group
Page 54: (top and middle left) Deen Van Meer
Page 54: (bottom and center) Disney Theatrical Group
Page 55: Kenneth Van Sickle
Page 56: (top) Christopher Oram
Page 56: (bottom) Disney Theatrical Group
Page 57: (top) Disney Theatrical Group
Page 57: (bottom) Deen Van Meer
Page 58: Disney Theatrical Group
Page 59: Deen Van Meer
Page 60: (top left and right) Christopher Oram
Page 60: (bottom left and right) Deen Van Meer
Page 61: (top right) Andrew Eccles
Page 61: (top left) Marc Brenner
Page 61: (bottom all) Deen Van Meer
Page 62: (top left and bottom left and right) Greg Barnes
Page 62: (left center and bottom center) Deen Van Meer
Page 63: (top right and bottom left) Deen Van Meer
Page 63: (top right and bottom right) Christopher Oram
Page 64: (top left) Marc Brenner
Page 64: (all others) Disney Theatrical Group
Page 65: Disney Theatrical Group
Page 66: Provided by Bobby Creighton
Page 67: top) Deen Van Meer
Page 67: (bottom left) Disney Theatrical Group
Page 67: (bottom right) Marc Brenner
Pages 68–69: Disney Theatrical Group
Page 70: (top right and bottom right) Phillip Jarrell
Page 70: (bottom left) Disney Theatrical Group
Page 71: Joan Marcus
Page 73: (top) Johann Persson
Page 73: (bottom) Joan Marcus
Page 74: Deen Van Meer
Page 75: Charles Erikson
Pages 76–77: Deen Van Meer
Pages 78–79: Deen Van Meer
Page 80: (left) Disney Theatrical Group
Page 80: (center) Marc Brenner
Page 81: Deen Van Meer
Page 82: (left) Disney Theatrical Group
Page 82: (right) Joan Marcus
Page 83: (top right) Disney Theatrical Group
Page 84: Marc Brenner
Page 85: Disney Theatrical Group
Page 86: Deen Van Meer
Page 87: (top left and right) Joan Marcus
Page 87: (bottom) Deen Van Meer
Page 88: (top left) Joan Marcus
Page 88: (center and bottom left) Deen Van Meer
Page 89: Marc Brenner
Page 90: (left) Provided by Mattea Conforti
Page 90: (bottom) Deen Van Meer
Pages 90–91: Provided by Mattea Conforti
Page 92: Deen Van Meer
Page 93: Deen Van Meer
Page 94: Marc Brenner

Page 95: (right) Deen Van Meer
Page 95: (top) Stock Photo
Page 96: Atsutoshi Shimosaka, Takashi Uehara, Ken Arai
Page 97: (top) James Morgan
Page 97: (bottom) Deen Van Meer
Page 98: Disney Theatrical Group
Page 99: Disney Theatrical Group
Pages 100–101: Marc Brenner
Page 102: Deen Van Meer
Page 103: (top and center) Joan Marcus
Page 103: (background) Gino Domenico
Page 104: Joan Marcus
Page 105: (top) Deen Van Meer
Page 105 (center left and center right) Kenneth Van Sickle
Page 105: (bottom) Deen Van Meer
Page 106: (top right and left) Marc Brenner
Page 106: (bottom right) Deen Van Meer
Page 107: Disney Theatrical Group
Page 108: (top left) Joan Marcus
Page 108: (insert) Courtesy of NK Productions, Inc.
Page 108: (center and bottom left) Deen Van Meer
Page 109: (left) Disney Theatrical Group
Page 109: (right) Deen Van Meer
Page 109: (bottom) Courtesy of NK Productions, Inc.
Page 110: Courtesy of NK Productions, Inc.
Page 111: (top) Courtesy of NK Productions, Inc.
Page 111: (bottom) Marc Brenner
Page 112: (top left and right and bottom left) Joan Marcus
Page 112: (bottom right) Courtesy of NK Productions, Inc.
Page 113: (top) Deen Van Meer
Page 113: (bottom) Dusty Bennett
Page 114: (top and center) Joan Marcus
Page 114: (bottom) Deen Van Meer
Page 115: (top) Disney Theatrical Productions
Page 115: (bottom) Jim Carmody
Page 115: (center) Joan Marcus
Page 116: (top left) Joan Marcus
Page 116: (bottom left) Matt Carr
Page 116: (center) Deen Van Meer
Page 117: (top) Deen Van Meer
Page 117: (bottom) Joan Marcus
Page 118: (top) Deen Van Meer
Page 118: (bottom) Joan Marcus
Page 119: Joan Marcus
Page 120: (center) Provided by Anne Quart
Page 120: (background) Rob Halliday
Page 121: (bottom) Disney Theatrical Group
Page 121: (top) Provided by Lisa Dawn Cave
Page 123: (left) Dusty Bennett
Page 123: (right) Disney Theatrical Group
Page 124: Deen Van Meer
Page 125: © iStockphoto.com/aheinzen
Pages 126–127: Jesuit High School
Page 128: (top) Medford Memorial Middle School
Page 128: (bottom) Flagship Summer Theatre
Page 129: (top) McAuliffe International School
Page 129: (center) Gwendolyn Brooks Middle School
Page 129: (bottom) Harlem School of the Arts
Page 131: (top left) Hull Jackson Montessori
Page 131: (top right) Jesuit High School
Page 131: (bottom left) Jesuit High School
Page 131: (bottom center) Bradford High School
Page 131: (bottom right) Jesuit High School
Pages 134–135: Floyd Central High School
Page 136: Children's Musical Theatreworks
Page 137: Bradford High School
Page 139: Joan Marcus
Page 140: Matt Furman
Page 141: Ken Martinez
Page 142-143: (Playbills): From PLAYBILL. Copyright © 1994, 1997, 2000, 2006, 2008, 2012, 2014, 2015, 2016 and 2018. Reprinted by permission of Playbill, Inc.

Acknowledgments

The list of people who appear in this book and helped along the way is deep, and we are grateful to each and every one of them. And of course, the Disney Theatrical Group team in New York and around the world are responsible for extraordinary magic every day and I'm deeply indebted to them.

My thanks go to Wendy Lefkon for endless permission, support, guidance, and intelligence, the entire team from the first edition who set the path, most especially Dusty Bennett who pushed so hard back in the day. This edition would never have happened without Steve Downing, Max Garvin, Al Giuliani, Greg Josken, and, of course, Matthew White for nurturing, and supporting, and tolerating. Most of all, my thanks goes to Jeff Kurtti, who for thirty-five years has provided endless repartee, boundless encouragement, a whack on the head with a rolled-up newspaper when required, and the words that made this book possible, "When do we start?"

In addition, this book wouldn't have happened without the cooperation and support of the following people: Jane Abramson, Caitlin Baird, Caley Beretta, Hunter Chancellor, Brandon Fake, Andrew Flatt, Anne Quart, Clifford Schwartz, David Scott, Kristin Stewart, Seth Stuhl, Winnie Ho, Warren Meislin, Kate Milford, Rachel Rivera, and Monica Vasquez.

ABOUT THE AUTHORS

THOMAS SCHUMACHER was born in California sometime during the past century. Before computers or fax machines. Before video games or color television. Before CDs or DVDs —but during previews for the original production of *The Music Man* on Broadway. That's all anyone needs to know about that.

Like all kids who can read well out loud, he thought he was an actor. It turned out he wasn't much of an actor, but his love for theater led him to do everything else backstage and in the front of house.

He has made his living at one time or another as a shoe salesman, costume dyer, actor, gift wrapper, director, busboy, production assistant, kitchen worker, box-office treasurer, custodian, film executive, driver, teacher, puppeteer, movie producer, playground leader, stage carpenter, sound operator, sandwich maker, stage manager, personal assistant to a famous actress, and most recently, Broadway producer.

On Broadway for Disney, he has produced *King David*, *The Lion King*, Elton John and Tim Rice's *Aida*, *Tarzan*®, *Mary Poppins* with Cameron Mackintosh, *Newsies*, *Aladdin*, *Peter and the Starcatcher*, and *Frozen*. On tour, he produced *On The Record*, a collection of Disney songs, as well as a stage version of *The Hunchback of Notre Dame* and *Freaky Friday*. His shows have been seen outside of Broadway in major cities like London, Toronto, Hamburg, Amsterdam, Tokyo, Seoul, Sydney, Melbourne, and Shanghai, and on various tours throughout the United States and abroad.

Also for Disney, he produced the animated film *The Rescuers Down Under* and was executive producer of the film *The Lion King*. For Disney Animation he also supervised the development and production of some twenty feature films, including *Mulan, Lilo and Stitch, Pocahontas, Tarzan*®, and *The Nightmare Before Christmas*.

Before all of that, he worked for a ballet company, did everything anyone asked at the Mark Taper Forum, was a staff producer on the 1984 Olympic Arts Festival, and brought Cirque du Soleil to America for the very first time as part of the Los Angeles Festival. He went to school at the University of California, Los Angeles, where he studied theater and dreamed of getting to do it for a living.

He lives in New York.

JEFF KURTTI was born in Seattle, and from day one, it seemed, was destined to work for Disney. Jeff, too, thought he was an actor, but when he grew up and stopped being cute and precocious, acting was out—but he still followed the Disney path.

Over the years, he has worked as a movie theater usher, a publicist, a graphic artist, a personal assistant to an arts executive, a Walt Disney Imagineer, and a Walt Disney Company marketing rep. Soon he found that he could write books about the things he liked, and other people would be interested and pay him to do it!

He is the author of books like *The Great Movie Musical Trivia Book, The Art of "Mulan," The Art of Disneyland, Travels with Walt Disney, The Disney Christmas Card,* and *Practically Poppins in Every Way.*

Jeff also took a stab at making video productions, and got to work on DVD collector's editions of great movies like *Around the World in 80 Days, The Adventures of Robin Hood, The Lord of the Rings: The Fellowship of the Ring, Tarzan, Toy Story, Fantasia, Snow White and the Seven Dwarfs, Beauty and the Beast,* and a large portion of the *Walt Disney Treasures* DVD edition series with Leonard Maltin.

For a time, he did everything anyone asked him to at the Paramount Theatre and the 5th Avenue Theatre in Seattle before moving to Los Angeles, where he worked on the 1984 Olympic Arts Festival. It was there that he met a young staff producer who became a lasting and loyal friend and supporter, and an all-around fun and favorite guy—Thomas Schumacher.

Jeff lives in Claremont, California, with four of his other fun and favorite guys: Kenneth, Brendan, Joseph, and Mitchell.

These are opening night title pages from the shows discussed in this book. All the names of the creative teams and the casts are shown here. I always save programs to look back and see who did what.

THE PROGRAM

Disney
PRESENTS

THE LION KING

Music & Lyrics by
ELTON JOHN & TIM RICE

Additional Music & Lyrics by
LEBO M. MARK MANCINA, JAY RIFKIN, JULIE TAYMOR, HANS ZIMMER

Book by
ROGER ALLERS & IRENE MECCHI

Starring

JOHN VICKERY

GEOFF HOYLE   TSIDII LE LOKA   SAMUEL E. WRIGHT

JASON RAIZE   TOM ALAN ROBBINS

STANLEY WAYNE MATHIS   TRACY NICOLE CHAPMAN   HEATHER HEADLEY

SCOTT IRBY-RANNIAR   KEVIN CAHOON

KAJUANA SHUFORD

and

MAX CASELLA

KEVIN BAILEY   EUGENE BARRY-HILL   GINA BREEDLOVE   CAMILLE M. BROWN   IRESOL CARDONA
ALBERTO CRUZ, Jr.   MAIIK ALLAN DAVIS   LINDIWE DLAMINI   NTOMB KHONA DLAMINI   SHEILA GIBBS
LANA GORDON   LINDIWE HLENGWA   TIMOTHY HUNTER   CHRISTOPHER JACKSON   JENNIFER JOSEPHS
VANESSA A. JONES   SAM McKELTON   MICHAEL JOY   PACA KULU   RON KUNENE   SONYA LESLIE   AUBREY LYNCH II
PHILIP DORIAN McADOO   PETER ANTHONY MOORE   NANDI MORAKE   NHLANHLA NGEMA
KARINE PLANTADIT-BAGEOT   DANNY RUTIGLIANO   LEVENSKY SMITH   ASHI K. SMYTHE
ENDALYN TAYLOR-SHELLMAN   RACHEL TECORA TUCKER   FRANK WRIGHT II   CHRISTINE YASUNAGA   and LEBO M

Adapted from the screenplay by
IRENE MECCHI & JONATHAN ROBERTS & LINDA WOOLVERTON

| *Scenic Design* | *Costume Design* | *Lighting Design* | *Mask & Puppet Design* |
| RICHARD HUDSON | JULIE TAYMOR | DONALD HOLDER | JULIE TAYMOR & MICHAEL CURRY |

| *Sound Design* | *Hair & Makeup Design* | | *Casting* |
| TONY MEOLA | MICHAEL WARD | | JAY BINDER |

| *Technical Director* | *Production Stage Manager* | | *Press Representative* |
| DAVID BENKEN | JEFF LEE | | BONEAU/BRYAN-BROWN |

| *Music Director* | *Orchestrators* | | *Music Coordinator* |
| JOSEPH CHURCH | ROBERT ELHAI DAVID METZGER BRUCE FOWLER | | MICHAEL KELLER |

OPENING NIGHT: MAY 10, 2006

RICHARD RODGERS THEATRE

UNDER THE DIRECTION OF JAMES M. NEDERLANDER AND JAMES L. NEDERLANDER

DISNEY THEATRICAL PRODUCTIONS
under the direction of
Thomas Schumacher
presents

TARZAN

Music and Lyrics by
PHIL COLLINS

Book by
DAVID HENRY HWANG

with

JOSH STRICKLAND   JENN GAMBATESE
MERLE DANDRIDGE   CHESTER GREGORY II
TIM JEROME   DONNIE KESHAWARZ
DANIEL MANCHE   ALEX RUTHERFORD

and

SHULER HENSLEY

DARRIN BAKER   MARCUS BELLAMY   CELINA CARVAJAL   DWAYNE CLARK   VERONICA deSOYZA
KEARRAN GIOVANNI   MICHAEL HOLLICK   JOSHUA KOBAK   KARA MADRID   KEVIN MASSEY
ANASTACIA McCLESKEY   RIKA OKAMOTO   MARLYN ORTIZ   WHITNEY OSENTOSKI   JOHN ELLIOTT OYZON
ANDY PELLICK   ANGELA PHILLIPS   STEFAN RAULSTON   HORACE V. ROGERS   SEAN SAMUELS
NICK SANCHEZ   NIKI SCALERA   NATALIE SILVERLIEB   JO AUBREY SMITH   RACHEL STERN

Based on the story Tarzan of the Apes by
EDGAR RICE BURROUGHS
and the Disney film Tarzan
Screenplay by
TAB MURPHY, BOB TZUDIKER & NONI WHITE
Directed by
KEVIN LIMA & CHRIS BUCK

| *Scenic and Costume Design* | | *Lighting Design* |
| BOB CROWLEY | | NATASHA KATZ |

| *Sound Design* | *Hair Design* | *Make-Up Design* |
| JOHN SHIVERS | DAVID BRIAN BROWN | NAOMI DONNE |

| | *Soundscape* | *Fight Direction* |
| | LON BENDER | RICK SORDELET |

| | *Dance Arrangements* | *Orchestrations* |
| | JIM ABBOTT | DOUG BESTERMAN |

| *Music Coordinator* | | *Casting* |
| MICHAEL KELLER | | BERNARD TELSEY CASTING |

| *Technical Supervisor* | | *Press Representative* |
| TOM SHANE BUSSEY | | BONEAU/BRYAN-BROWN |

| | *Associate Producer* | |
| | MARSHALL B. PURDY | |

Aerial Design by
... ICHÓN BALDINU

Music Produced by
PAUL BOGAEV

Choreographed by
MERYL TANKARD

OPENING NIGHT: APRIL 18, 1994

PALACE THEATRE

OWNED AND OPERATED BY STEWART F. LANE
AND THE MESSRS. NEDERLANDER

Walt Disney Productions
presents

SUSAN EGAN   and   TERRENCE MANN
in

Disney's

Beauty and the Beast

Music by		*Book by*
ALAN MENKEN	HOWARD ASHMAN & TIM RICE	LINDA WOOLVERTON
	Lyrics by	

with

BURKE MOSES   GARY BEACH   BETH FOWLER   HEATH LAMBERTS
ELEANOR GLOCKNER   STACEY LOGA...   ... DRESS   KENNY RASKIN

JOAN BARBER   ROXANE BARLOW   HA...
KATE DOWE   DAVID ELDER   MERWIN FOAR...
KIM HUBER   ELMORE JAMES   ALISA I...
BARBARA MARINEAU   JOANNE McHU...
BILL NABEL   WENDY OLIVER   VINCE PESCE...
GORDON STANLEY   LINDA TALCOTT   ...

TOM BO...

| *Scenic Design* | *Orchestra-D...* |
| STAN MEYER | ANN HOULD... |

| *Sound Design* | *Hair...* |
| T. RICHARD FITZGERALD | DAVID H. LAW... |

| *Production Supervision* | |
| DODGER PRODUCTIONS | JEREMIAH J. HARRI... |

| *Casting* | *Musical Arr...* |
| JAY BINDER | GLEN KELLY |

Orchestrators	
DANNY TROOB	DAVID FR...
	MATT...

ROBERT J...

OPENING NIGHT: MARCH 23, 2000

PALACE THEATRE

OWNED AND OPERATED BY STEWART F. LANE
AND THE MESSRS. NEDERLANDER

HYPERION THEATRICALS
under the direction of
Peter Schneider and Thomas Schumacher
presents

AIDA

| *Music by* | *Lyrics by* |
| ELTON JOHN | TIM RICE |

Book by
LINDA WOOLVERTON
and
ROBERT FALLS & DAVID HENRY HWANG

SUGGESTED BY THE OPERA

Starring

HEATHER HEADLEY   ADAM PASCAL   SHERIE RENÉ SCOTT
JOHN HICKOK   DAMIAN PERKINS
TYREES ALLEN   DANIEL ORESKES

ROBERT M. ARMITAGE   TROY ALLAN BURGESS   FRANNE CALMA
CHRIS PAYNE DUPRÉ   THURSDAY FARRAR   KELLI FOURNIER   BOB GAYNOR
KISHA HOWARD   TIM HUNTER   YOUN KIM   KYRIA LITTLE   KENYA UNIQUE MASSE...
CORINNE McFADDEN   PHINEAS NEWBORN III   JODY RIPPLINGER   RAYMOND RODRI...
ERIC SCIOTTO   TIMOTHY EDWARD SMITH   ENDALYN TAYLOR-SHELLMAN
SAMUEL N. THIAM   VINCENT   SCHELE WILLIAMS   NATALIA ZISA

| *Scenic & Costume Design* | | *Lighting Design* |
| BOB CROWLEY | | NATASHA KATZ |

| *Sound Design* | *Hair Design* | *Makeup...* |
| STEVE C. KENNEDY | DAVID BRIAN BROWN | NAOMI ... |

| *Music Produced and Musical Direction by* | *Music Arrangements* | *Orches...* |
| PAUL BOGAEV | GUY BABYLON PAUL BOGAEV | STEVE MA... GUY BA... PAUL B... |

| *Music Coordinator* | *Dance Arrangements* | *Technical...* |
| MICHAEL KELLER | BOB GUSTAFSON JIM ABBOTT GARY SELIGSON | THEATERS... |

| *Development Casting* | *Casting* | *Fight D...* |
| JAY BINDER | BERNARD TELSEY CASTING | RICK SO... |

| *Associate Producer* | *Press Representative* | *Production S...* |
| MARSHALL B. PURDY | BONEAU/BRYAN-BROWN | CLIFFORD... |

Choreography by
WAYNE CILENTO

Directed by
ROBERT FALLS

Originally developed at the Alliance Theatre Company in Atlanta, Geo...

Disney's

THE HUNCHBACK OF NOTRE DAME

| *Music by* | *Lyrics by* | |
| ALAN MENKEN | STEPHEN SCHWARTZ | PE... |

Based on the novel by Victor Hugo with songs from the D...

Starring (in alphabetical order)

MICHAEL ARDEN   ERIK LIBERMAN   PATR...
CIARA RENÉE   ANDREW SAMONSK...

and with JULIAN DECKER   MARY JOE DUGGAN   IAN PATRICK GIB...
SAMANTHA MASSELL   NEAL MAYER   NORA MENKEN   WILLIAM MI...
VINCENT RODRIGUEZ III   RICHARD RUIZ   JOSEPH J. SIMEONE   JEREMY...

| *Scenic Design* | *Costume Design* | |
| ALEXANDER DODGE | ALEJO VIETTI | |

| *Sound Design* | *Hair & Wig Design* | |
| GARETH OWEN | CHARLES LAPOINTE | |

| *Casting* | *Flying by* | *Press Representative* |
| TARA RUBIN CASTING | FOY | SHAYNE A. MILLER |

| *Music Supervisor, Vocal & Incidental Music Arranger* | *Music Director* | *Orchestra...* |
| MICHAEL KOSARIN | BRENT-ALAN HUFFMAN | MICHAEL ST... |

| | *Production S...* | |
| | CLIFFORD... | |

Choreographed by
CHASE BROCK

Directed by
SCOTT SCHWARTZ

OPENING NIGHT: MARCH 20, 2014

NEW AMSTERDAM THEATRE

Disney Theatrical Productions
under the direction of
Thomas Schumacher
presents

Disney
Aladdin
BROADWAY'S NEW MUSICAL COMEDY

| *Music by* | *Lyrics by* | *Book and Additional Lyrics by* |
| ALAN MENKEN | HOWARD ASHMAN and TIM RICE | CHAD BEGUELIN |

Based on the Disney film written by RON CLEMENTS, JOHN MUSKER, TED ELLIOTT & TERRY ROSSIO and directed and produced by JOHN MUSKER & RON CLEMENTS

Starring

ADAM JACOBS
JAMES MONROE IGLEHART   COURTNEY REED
BRIAN GONZALES   BRANDON O'NEILL   JONATHAN SCHWARTZ
CLIFTON DAVIS   DON DARRYL RIVERA
MERWIN FOARD   MICHAEL JAMES SCOTT

and

JONATHAN FREEMAN
as "Jafar"

TIA ALTINAY   MIKE CANNON   ANDREW CAO   LAUREN CIARDULLO   JOSHUA DELA CRUZ
YUREL ECHEZABRETA   DAISY HOBBS   DONALD JONES, JR.   ADAM KAOKEPT   NIKKI LONG   STANLEY MARTIN
BRANDT MARTINEZ   MICHAEL MINDLIN   RHEA PATTERSON   BOBBY PESTKA   KHORI MICHELLE PETINAUD   ALDIS PEVEC
ARIEL REID   JENNIFER RIAS   TRENT SAUNDERS   JAZ SEALEY   DENNIS STOWE   MARISHA WALLACE   BUD WEBER

| *Associate Producer* | *Technical Supervision* | *Production Supervisor* |
| ANNE QUART | GEOFFREY QUART/ HUDSON THEATRICAL ASSOCIATES DAVID BENKEN | CLIFFORD SCHWARTZ |

| *Production Managers* | *Associate Director* | *Associate Choreographer* | *Casting* |
| MYRIAH BASH EDUARDO CASTRO | SCOTT TAYLOR | JOHN MacINNIS | TARA RUBIN CASTING ERIC WOODALL, CSA |

| | *Dance Music Arrangements* | *Music Coordinator* | *Fight Direction* |
| | GLEN KELLY | HOWARD JOINES | J. ALLEN SUDDETH |

| *Sound Design* | *Hair Design* | *Makeup Design* | *Illusion Design* |
| KEN TRAVIS | JOSH MARQUETTE | MILAGROS MEDINA-CERDEIRA | JIM STEINMEYER |

| | *Costume Design* | *Lighting Design* | |
| | GREGG BARNES | NATASHA KATZ | |

| | *Scenic Design* | | |
| | BOB CROWLEY | | |

| | *Orchestrations* | | |
| | DANNY TROOB | | |

| | *Music Supervision, Incidental Music & Vocal Arrangements* | | |
| | MICHAEL KOSARIN | | |

Directed and Choreographed by
CASEY NICHOLAW

The premiere of Aladdin was produced by The 5th Avenue Theatre in Seattle, WA. David Armstrong, Executive Producer & Artistic Director, Bernadine C. Griffin, Managing Director, Bill Berry, Producing Director.